BASICS

DESIGN

Gavin Ambrose
Paul Harris

TYPOGRAPHY

Second Edition

Bloomsbury Visual Arts
An imprint of Bloomsbury Publishing Plc

B L O O M S B U R Y
LONDON · OXFORD · NEW YORK · NEW DELHI · SYDNEY

Bloomsbury Visual Arts
An imprint of Bloomsbury Publishing Plc

Imprint previously known as AVA Publishing

50 Bedford Square   1385 Broadway
London   New York
WC1B 3DP   NY 10018
UK   USA

www.bloomsbury.com

BLOOMSBURY and the Diana logo are trademarks of Bloomsbury Publishing Plc

First published by AVA Publishing SA, 2005
This 2nd edition is published by Bloomsbury Visual Arts, an imprint of Bloomsbury Publishing Plc
Copyright © Bloomsbury Publishing Plc, 2017

Gavin Ambrose has asserted his right under the Copyright, Designs and Patents Act, 1988, to be identified as Author of this work.

British Library Cataloguing-in-Publication Data
A catalogue record for this book is available from the British Library.

ISBN: PB: 978-1-4742-2528-1
         ePDF: 978-1-4742-2529-8

Library of Congress Cataloging-in-Publication Data
Names: Ambrose, Gavin, author. | Harris, Paul, 1971- author.
Title: Typography / Gavin Ambrose and Paul Harris
Description: Second edition. | London ; New York : Bloomsbury Visual Arts, [2017] |
Series: Basics design | Includes bibliographical references and index.
Identifiers: LCCN 2016029278 (print) | LCCN 2016037579 (ebook) | ISBN
9781474225281 (paperback) | ISBN 9781474225298 (ePDF)
Subjects: LCSH: Graphic design (Typography) | Type and type-founding. |
BISAC: DESIGN / Graphic Arts / Typography. | DESIGN / Graphic Arts /
General.
Classification: LCC Z246 .A558 2017 (print) | LCC Z246 (ebook) | DDC
686.2/2--dc23
LC record available at https://lccn.loc.gov/2016029278

Series: Basics Design
Cover design: Louise Dugdale
Cover image: Sutchinda Rangsi Thompson

Typeset by Gavin Ambrose
Printed and bound in China

To find out more about our authors and books visit www.bloomsbury.com. Here you will find extracts, author interviews, details of forthcoming events and the option to sign up for our newsletters.

02 Defying Gravity

Official science has curbed life and mobility because many of its enthusiasts buy into better systems

Client: Sony
Design: Intro
Typographic summary: Dot-matrix typeface set to convey a sense of speed

03 06

Gravity is not a force.

Document 1. The theory of anti-gravity as a psychological flight path

3G MAGLEV

Defying Gravity

This booklet, created by Intro design studio, accompanied the launch of the *Wipeout Fusion*; a game for Sony's Playstation 2. The dot-matrix typeface used is erratically typeset and the use of overprinting, bleeds and different column configurations all contribute towards reflecting the frenetic sense of movement that the game has.

Planning Unit

Blok Design

Triboro

Studio Myerscough

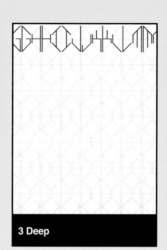

3 Deep

KesselsKramer

Typography | Contents

Typography is the means by which a written idea is given a visual form. Due to the volume and variety of typefaces available the selection of the components of this visual form can dramatically affect the readability of the idea and a reader's feelings towards it. Typography is one of the most influential elements on the character and emotional quality of a design. It can produce a neutral effect or rouse the passions, it can symbolize artistic, political or philosophical movements, or it can express the personality of an individual or organization.

Typefaces vary from clear and distinguishable letterforms that flow easily before the eye, and so are suitable for extended blocks of text, to those more dramatic and eye-catching typefaces that grab attention and so are used in headlines and advertisements.

Typography is anything but static and continues to evolve. Many typefaces in current use find their foundations in designs created during earlier historical epochs. This second edition provides a brief history of type to provide some historical context to facilitate the understanding of the development of type and includes new material, interviews and exercises to show how the use of typography continues to evolve and progress in both print and digital.

Looking at Type

Definitions of some of the most common typographical terms are explained, providing a basic understanding of letterforms and typography. Although often named after superseded technologies, these terms are still in general use and particularly relevant.

Type Classification

A sound understanding of how typefaces are classified is crucial for the modern designer. It is necessary in order to appreciate the historical relevance of type and to recognize the nuances of available type forms.

Choosing Type

Type choices play a key role in establishing the voice of a design or brand and this section examines some of the aspects behind the choice of a typeface.

Setting Type

Exploring how type can be measured and manipulated facilitates a level of control and finesse. Basic techniques and structures are explained to help a designer use type effectively.

Type Generation

Many pieces of work require bespoke typographical solutions, often these will include the adjustment of existing typefaces or the generation of new ones.

Type Realization

The realization or placement of type can dramatically add to the effectiveness and intensity of a design. Considerations of paper stocks and printing techniques can profoundly enhance a finished design and the examples contained within this section serve to demonstrate this.

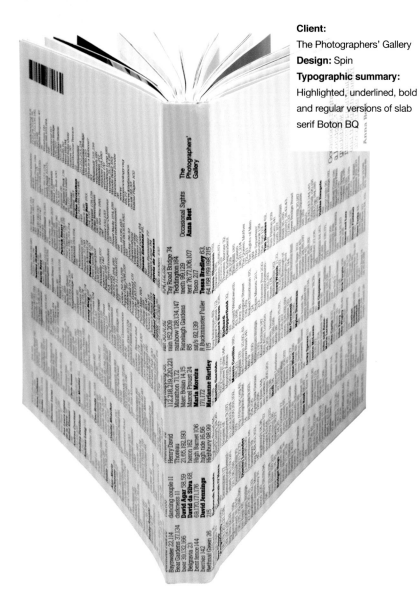

Client:
The Photographers' Gallery
Design: Spin
Typographic summary:
Highlighted, underlined, bold
and regular versions of slab
serif Boton BQ

Occasional Sights

Occasional Sights is a guidebook to London, created by artist Anna Best, which explores missed opportunities and things that do not really exist in the UK capital. The design by Spin features a cover that also serves as a complete index to the book's contents; something more commonly contained within the closing pages of a publication. The index uses highlighted, underlined, bold and regular versions of Boton BQ, an Egyptian slab serif typeface. This typeface closely mimics the character impressions made by a typewriter and is traditionally used to compensate for coarse printing stocks and low-grade printing.

A Brief History of Type

The ability to record language, to put words on paper, represented a fundamental leap in the development of humankind, and ultimately in the democratization of information and learning. Today, people in the developed world are so used to writing on electronic devices that some would argue the ability to handwrite is declining and grammatical standards are being sacrificed for conciseness of communication.

It is a relatively well-known fact that Johannes Gutenburg invented the printing press in 1439 and is considered the father of the printed word. Less well-known is the fact that a printing system was working in China and Korea long before Gutenburg. As such, reproduction of the written word can be considered as one of the first processes to be industrialized allowing for its massification. The other innovation of Gutenburg was that he published in the vernacular language rather than Latin, which meant his books could be read more widely, generating a class of people used to reading books other than the elitist Latin productions of the Bible that until then had been common. Merchants of the time such as William Caxton, who introduced the printing press into England, where quick to see the commercial potential of printing and helped accelerate its spread. That said, printed works were still a luxury item until the industrial revolution really allowed the printed word to reach the masses.

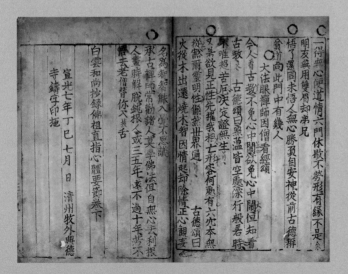

Above: Pictured is a spread from the Gutenberg Bible held by the British Library, London, UK.

Left: Pictured is a spread from *Selected Teachings of Buddhist Sages and Son Masters* by Jikji held by Bibliothèque Nationale de France, the earliest known book printed with movable metal type that was printed in Korea in 1377.

Typography | A Brief History of Type

Early typefaces were based on the handwritten characters that they replaced and reflected the characteristics of national writing styles. Hence, early typefaces mimicked the heavy German letterforms that were subsequently called gothic, while in Italy, the finer, more cursive letterforms were prevalent and became known as italics.

For the purposes of this book, and particularly this introduction, the development of the mechanical, industrial printing press is the key point in time, as that is when many of the terms and concepts that we associate with type and its rich language became codified.

Industrial production also facilitated the development of an increasing number of typefaces and styles as well as the rise of the type foundries that had their apogee in the first half of the twentieth century such as Monotype – the casting of single characters – and Linotype – the casting of whole lines of characters and hot metal typesetting that injected molten type metal into a mold with the shape of one or more glyphs.

A composing stick on which passages of type are arranged, lying upon a case of movable type.

 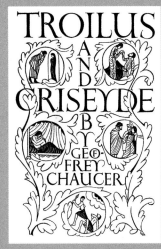

Pictured (left) is a monotype printer at work in the Co-operative Wholesale Society's printing works at Pelaw, Durham in 1929. Pictured (right) is the title page for the Geoffrey Chaucer poem *Troilus and Criseyde* created in 1927 by Eric Gill for Golden Cockerel Press.

Creating typefaces and typesetting were crafts that took years of apprenticeship to develop and master. This period saw a number of master craftsmen at work, some of whom pushed typography into new directions; individuals who are now considered legendary such as Giambattista Bodoni, Eric Gill and Adrian Frutiger. Frutiger's work is referenced in this book and his innovations such as the development of sans serif typefaces and the grid system of typeface classification are still in use today.

The second half of the twentieth century saw the development of graphic design as a distinct discipline in its own right and the codification of graphic design concepts. Nineteenth century posters often contained a broad mix of typeface styles, sizes, rules and other features that now, following the development of graphic design as a discipline, may seem messy and disorganized. One of the lasting contributions of this age is the rich and deep language that developed around typography to allow designers to communicate very precisely about every aspect of type with printers and other professionals, and increasingly the client, with terms such as line weight, line width, hairline serifs, bowl, leading, kerning, x-height, baseline and orientation.

It is worth noting that as the graphic design discipline has progressed it has become an increasingly present factor in our lives and as such we have become more sophisticated consumers of graphic design and typography.

Typography | A Brief History of Type

The current chapter of type can be said to originate in London in 1982 when media tycoon Rupert Murdoch's News International made the seismic transition from traditional hot metal to automated printing, making various traditional print shop roles obsolete overnight. It did not take many years following this for two centuries of newspaper printing in the famous Fleet Street to come to an end and relocate to London's Docklands.

Personal computers today come with dozens of typefaces as standard, giving people access to a quantity of different styles and ways of expressing themselves that was unthinkable a generation ago, when using a different typeset probably meant having to physically purchase a new box of characters. A visit to the local printer to get some business cards would have meant a choice between Times New Roman, Helvetica or another of the limited range of typefaces the printer had for his letterpress machine. Information technology has made the design, development and distribution of typefaces relatively simple and much quicker, allowing many more people to become type designers, arguably deskilling the role of the typographer in the process.

The development of type designing software allows people, experts and non-experts alike to create new type styles from scratch or to tweak existing type into new forms in a relatively short period of time, marking the full democratization of the type creation process. The number of typefaces has increased exponentially allowing for greater personalization of communication and branding. This is one of the biggest threats to typography as a profession, akin in its way to the printing revolution unleashed by Rupert Murdoch in 1982. However, the deskilling and democratization of type design also results in a general lowering of typographic standards and this represents a big opportunity for contemporary designers. The prevalence of dumbed-down typography created and set by those with very little idea of its fundamentals means that there is always a space for professionals who have the ability to set type beautifully to stand out and create communications that are both relevant and unique.

While the processes for the creation, distribution and reproduction of type have changed beyond recognition, the industrial language of type has survived and thrives, with the digital age even making certain terms part of the common, shared language of everyday people pretty much anyone who can use a computer knows what bold or italic means. Those who pay more attention to their word processors will also know strikethrough, underlining, superscript and even ligatures and those who open up and become familiar with the publishing software become familiar with an array of typographical terminology. This text is but a much-abridged history of type that is intended to bring the reader to look at current typographic practice and trends, bearing in mind its historical context and development.

What of the future of type? Typographers continue to exist although type specialists are becoming increasingly rare as type design becomes another skill set that is absorbed into the abilities of that jack-of-all-trades, the graphic designer. While general typography is becoming accessible to more and more people, there is a resurgence in demand for bespoke typography that can give an identity to organizations in an ever increasingly visually-saturated world. The delivery of communication has changed; it is becoming more fluid and responsive. With communications simultaneously functioning over print (often print on demand), web and environmental mediums, the role of contemporary graphic design is changing and evolving. Typography, the presentation of the written word, remains a cornerstone in the ability to communicate information and share ideas, and should be treated with the importance it deserves.

Danish Tattooing
Pictured is the cover of Danish Tattooing by Jon Nordstrøm that features a simple, clean sans serif font. The cover, by Designbolaget, celebrates the simple use and power of typography.

Typography | A Brief History of Type

Client: Royal Academy of Arts
Design: Why Not Associates
Typographic summary:
Logotype with infilled counters,
specifically designed for the
exhibition's promotional
material

ROYAL ACADEMY OF ARTS
PICCADILLY W1

APOCALYPSE

BEAUTY AND HORROR IN CONTEMPORARY ART

23 SEPTEMBER-15 DECEMBER 2000
DAILY 10am-6pm FRIDAYS UNTIL 8.30pm
www.royalacademy.org.uk

Chapter 1

Looking at type

Typography contains a wealth of specialized terminology that designers and printers use when describing typefaces and their associated characteristics. While each term has a specific meaning, over time some have become distorted and otherwise altered by common usage. For example, many people incorrectly refer to 'obliques' as 'italics' simply because they both slant.

Many terms, such as 'leading' or 'em rule', originate from the hot metal printing industry that, until the explosion of information technology, was the bastion of typography. Many terms – including the names given to individual parts of a single character – are even older and originate in stonemasonry.

This chapter will introduce and define some common typographical terms used to describe a typeface, as well as their synonyms and alternative, distorted uses. An understanding of typographic terminology will enable the reader to discuss, specify and communicate typographic requirements with clients, designers and industry professionals and provide a deeper understanding of the subject.

We should welcome typographic variety as the natural consequence of human creativity. Sebastian Carter

Apocalypse

This poster was created by Why Not Associates for the *Apocalypse* show at the Royal Academy of Arts in London. Beauty and horror are visually expressed via the harsh juxtaposition of the apocalyptic typography that cuts into the serene image. The removal of the counters from the letters dehumanizes them, implying sinister overtones. The typography appears in a simple, traditional hierarchy that is also subverted by the apocalyptic title.

Where type is used

Type is everywhere. It is on almost everything we buy, on the pages of books and magazines, on walls, floors and street signs. To a greater or lesser extent, all type used to be printed, but now type is used and has to function (be legible and readable) across various different platforms such as screens both large and small, and the ever-growing digital space.

There are many typeface varieties and each one possesses a distinct personality. Some typefaces are formal and convey a sense of authority, while others are more relaxed and appear to be less structured. Typeface usage can therefore tell a reader as much about the originator of the communication as the message itself.

However, in addition to choosing the right type personality for a job, a designer must also consider the practical aspects of where the type will be used, as different platforms impose different performance requirements on a type. Typefaces may look different on a smartphone screen than on a printed brochure.

Kunsten Museum of Modern Art

Pictured is printed material created by Designbolaget for an exhibition at the Kunsten Museum of Modern Art that shows some of the various pieces that type in a design is used on, including a brochure, poster and invitation.

Client: Kunsten Museum
of Modern Art
Design: Designbolaget
Typographic summary:
Type used across various
pieces

What is type?

Typographer Eric Gill noted that 'letters are things, they are not pictures of things'. Letters represent the sounds of a spoken language and visually express ideas so that another person can understand them in the manner intended.

Typography concerns the setting of letters within a design for print or screen. The variety of typefaces and ways they can be used within a design, can enhance or alter the meaning of the words that type creates. The style in which letters are formed and presented alters our perceptions of the ideas they portray.

Modern

Russell Square
Designed for the Visual Graphics Corporation in 1973, it displays square-ish counterforms, reminiscent of early hi-tech developments.

Handwritten

Zapf Chancery
In contrast, Hermann Zapf's distinctive calligraphic typeface is based on chancery handwriting, developed during the Italian Renaissance.

Ornate

Küenstler Script
Reminiscent of intricate handwriting, Küenstler Script sacrifices a degree of legibility in favour of overall flair.

Simple

Gill Sans
Originally produced for the London & North Eastern Railway, here the emphasis is on legibility.

Futuristic

Eurostile
Aldo Novarese's seminal font reflects the optimism of 1950s' and 1960s' design.

Historical

Garamond
Evergreen font by Claude Garamond conveys a sense of classicism and historical importance.

Client: Arbuthnot Yon
Design: Planning Unit
Typographic summary:
Bespoke logotype, bold colors
and sans serif typography

Typography | What is type?

Arbuthnot Yon
Pictured are print elements for a brand identity for financial services recruitment company Arbuthnot Yon created by Planning Unit. The design aimed to bring a contemporary yet assertive voice to the company that participates in a very competitive field. Rather than use the clichéd stock photography that has saturated communications in the sector, it focused on a clear and honest approach through a bespoke logotype, bold colors and robust sans serif typography.

Cumbrae's

Pictured is store signage created by Blok Design as part of a brand identity redesign for high-end butcher shop Cumbrae's. Cumbrae's was one of the first to raise meats using natural practices and so the identity uses a sans serif font to juxtapose the brand's sense of swagger and innovation with a contemporary voice and presence.

Client: Cumbrae's
Design: Blok Design
Typographic summary:
Contemporary sans serif for
brand redesign

Typefaces and fonts (or founts)

In common usage, the words 'typeface' and 'font' are used synonymously. In most cases there is no harm in doing so as such substitution is virtually universal and most people, including designers, would be hard pressed to state each word's 'correct' definition if asked. However, each term does possess separate and quite distinct meanings.

According to James Felici's *Complete Manual of Typography*, a typeface is a collection of characters, letters, numbers, symbols, punctuation (and so on) that have the same, distinct design. A font however, is the physical means of typeface production, be it the description of a typeface in computer code, lithographic film, metal or woodcut. Felici explains this distinction in simple terms and describes the font as a cookie cutter and the typeface as the cookie produced from the cutter. When looking at a design, one can ask what typeface it uses or what font the type is set in, but strictly speaking, one cannot ask what font it uses.

Below left is the font (or cookie cutter) that is used to produce the typeface (or cookie) shown on the right.

Typeface

A typeface is
a collection of
characters, letters,
numbers, symbols,
punctuation (and
so on) that have a
distinct design.

Font (or fount)

A font (or fount) is
the physical means
used to create a
typeface, be it
computer code,
lithographic film,
metal or woodcut.

Typography | Typefaces and fonts (or founts)

Typeface style
A typeface family contains a range of different character styles, which can be applied to the same basic roman typeface.

This is illustrated below with the Helvetica Neue family. Roman is the basic cut and base style in which the majority of body text will be set. The other family members are variations of this and allow a designer greater flexibility to provide variation and emphasis, as and when required, to produce a more interesting and useful design, while preserving key typeface characteristics.

Roman

Helvetica Neue 55
Originates from inscriptions on Roman monuments.

Italic

Helvetica Neue 56
A version of the roman cut that slopes to the right.

Condensed

Helvetica Condensed
Condensed is a narrower version of the roman cut.

Extended

Helvetica Neue Extended
Extended is a wider version of the roman cut.

Boldface

Helvetica Neue 75
Uses a wider stroke than roman. Also called medium or black.

Light or thin

Helvetica Neue 35
A variation of the roman cut with a lighter stroke.

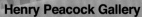

Henry Peacock Gallery

Jonathan Ellery, a founding partner of Browns, created this poster for an exhibition at London's Henry Peacock Gallery that features a quotation from boxer Muhammad Ali foil blocked into a reflective, metallic paper stock. This is an example of how print process choice can impact typeface choice. Here, a reverse out foil uses a condensed uppercase Helvetica bold typeface for legibility.

Client: Henry Peacock Gallery
Design: Browns
Typographic summary:
Helvetica bold condensed, upper case text block

I DONE WRASSLE AN ALLIGATOR, I TUSSLED WITH A WHALE. I DONE HANDCUFFED LIGHTNIN THROWN THUNDER IN JAIL. ONLY LAST WEEK THAT'S BAD, I MURDERED A ROCK, INJURED A STONE, HOSPITALIZED A BRICK, I'M SO MEAN I MAKE MEDICINE SICK.

Italic or oblique?

Although there is a distinction between italic and oblique typefaces, there is no right or wrong in their selection. As with all aspects of design, selection is based upon making an informed judgment about what works best for the piece.

Minion roman (left) / Minion italic (right)
The italic typeface is a true italic as it features redrawn characters.

Italics

A true italic is a drawn typeface based around an axis that is angled between 7–20 degrees. Italics have a calligraphic style and can sit compactly, in part due to their use of many ligatures. They are usually based upon serif typefaces. Notice the difference between the roman and italic characters shown above.

Helvetica Neue 75 (left) / Helvetica Neue 76 italic (right)
The italic variation is actually an oblique as it is redrawn to resemble the roman character.

Obliques

The 20th century saw typographers begin to develop slanted versions of roman characters, called obliques, as italics were not considered appropriate for the industrial and non-calligraphic designs of most sans serif typefaces. Oblique letterforms are essentially those of their roman counterparts but they are often incorrectly named italics.

Client: Barbican Gallery
Design: North
Typographic summary:
Futura Bold set on a
nine-degree slant

Barbican Gallery Literature

This brochure was created for the Barbican Arts Centre's Gallery by North design studio, and features a true italic version of Futura Bold that is set on a nine-degree slant, to counterbalance the effect of the italicization. The consistent use of a single typeface employed in a single fashion forms an integral part of the identity, in this instance the typography *is* the identity, as it is the unique setting of the type that becomes memorable and recognizable.

Looking at a typeface

Perhaps one of the most important things to keep in mind when looking at a typeface, or extended typeface family, is that each variation was originally created for a specific function.

The typeface is considered the base component for presenting a message as the examples below from the Minion typeface family demonstrate.

abcdefghijklmnopqrstuvwxyz

Minion Regular
The basic roman alphabet that is used for body text.

ABCDEFGHIJKLMNOPQRSTUVWXYZ

Minion Regular Caps
The standard capitals used for initials and headline text.

ABCDEFGHIJKLMNOPQRSTUVWXYZ

Minion Regular Small Caps
A special set of capitals for emphasizing specific text.

SMALL CAPS provide a designer with a subtle means of highlighting a section of text without it standing out too much and overpowering the surrounding body text. Titles, names and references can thus be distinguished without 'shouting' as they would if they were set in CAPITALS.

A SMALL CAP is far more harmonious with the body text because it has been specifically re-cut to have the same width strokes as the regular characters. This is not the case with ARTIFICIAL SMALL CAPS, which have strokes that look thin and give the impression that the characters have been elongated.

Blocks of text are considered easier to read when set in roman or old style (Antiqua), where there is a combination of majuscule and minuscule characters. This is because the human eye 'scans' the text using the ascenders and descenders to recognize words rather than reading each and every word. Majuscules share the same height and have fewer visual shortcuts for the eye than minuscules, which have ascending or descending stems that assist scanning.

TEXT SET IN MAJUSCULE CHARACTERS REQUIRES THE READER TO CONSTRUCT THE WORDS BY READING EACH INDIVIDUAL CHARACTER, WHICH CAN BE SLOW AND TIRING.

Lower case letters were developed by Alcuin in the 8th century, this development allowed text to be divided into sentences and paragraphs by opening the first word of a sentence with a capital letter.

Certain languages can look uncomfortable when set in roman. German, for example, uses initial capitals at the start of written nouns that disrupt the scanning of the eye: 'I went to the Shop in my Car to buy Food and a Book'.

Typography | Looking at a typeface

S P A C I N G
s p a c i n g

As lower case letters tend to flow into one another, it is considered bad typographical practice to letterspace them, as this makes the text more difficult to read. Capitals depend less on each other, and so we are more used to viewing and reading them with spacing in place.

Stroke

Refers specifically to the diagonal portion of letterforms such as 'N', 'M', or 'Y'. Stems, bars, arms, bowls etc. are collectively referred to as letterform strokes.

Stress

The direction in which a curved stroke changes weight.

Loop

The stroke that encloses or partially encloses a counter in a roman, i.e. double-storey 'g', that is connected to the bowl by a link. Sometimes used to describe the cursive 'p' and 'b'.

YT vaogpbG

Bracket

The curved portion of a serif that connects it to the stroke.

Hairline

The thinnest stroke in a typeface that has varying widths – can be clearly identified on a 'v' or 'a'.

Chin

Angled terminal part of the 'G'.

Apex

The point formed at the top of a character such as 'A', where the left and right strokes meet.

Shoulder or body

The arch formed on the 'h', 'n' etc.

Leg

The lower, down sloping stroke of the 'K', 'k' and 'R'. Sometimes used for the tail of a 'Q'.

Avhpd KYTF

Vertex

The angle formed at the bottom of a letter where the left and right strokes meet such as with the 'V'.

Ascenders and descenders

An ascender is the part of a letter that extends above the x-height; a descender falls below the baseline. Both of these are extenders.

Terminal

The terminal describes the finish of a stroke. Avenir contains a flat terminal, with no additional decoration. Variations include flared, convex, concave and rounded.

Tail

The descending stroke on the 'Q', 'K' or 'R'. The descenders on 'g', 'j', 'p', 'q', and 'y' may also be called tails as can the loop of the 'g'.

Link

The part that joins the two bowls of the double-storey 'g'.

Ear

Right side of the bowl of the 'g', the end of an 'r' or 'f' for example.

A Q s g f F

Serif

The small stroke at the end of a main vertical or horizontal stroke.

Spine

The left-to-right curving stroke in 'S' and 's'.

Arm, bar or crossbar

A horizontal stroke that is open at one or both ends as seen on the 'T', 'F', 'E' plus the upstroke on the 'K'.

Stem

The main vertical or diagonal stroke of a letter.

Crotch

Where the leg and arm of the 'K' and 'k' meet.

 T   K

Crossbar

A horizontal stroke on the 'A' and 'H'. A crossbar joins two stems together.

Cross stroke

The horizontal stroke on the characters 'A', 'H', 'T', 'e', 'f', 't'. This is sometimes called a crossbar. A cross stroke intersects a single stem.

Bowl / counter

The empty space inside the body stroke, which is surrounded by the bowl. The counter may be called an eye for the 'e'.

Typography | Typeface anatomy

X-height
The 'x-height' is a term applied to the distance between the baseline and the mean line of non-ascending or lower case letters.

The letter 'x' is used as a gauge because it is flat at both its top and bottom. The x-height is often used as a layout anchor to produce consistent positioning of images and text blocks. The x-height is a relative measure specific to the typeface in question. The physical measurement will differ from typeface to typeface even if the point size is the same; as shown in the examples opposite.

As different typefaces of the same point size have different x-heights an optical distortion can occur.

X-height variations between typefaces of the same point size create visual differences. For example, Folio (used here) has a comparatively large x-height, this means that less space appears between the lines and there is less room for ascenders and descenders than Cochin, which has a smaller x-height. This creates the illusion that there is less leading although it is identical.

As different typefaces of the same point size have different x-heights an optical distortion can occur.

X-height variations between typefaces of the same point size create visual differences. For example, Akzidenz Grotesk has a comparatively large x-height, this means that less space appears between the lines and there is less room for ascenders and descenders than say, Cochin (used here), which has a smaller x-height. This creates the illusion that there is less leading although it is identical.

Cap height ———————————————————————— Ascender height
Mean line ——————

RDLlpx

| X-height
Baseline ——————
Descender height ——————————————————————————

Cap height and ascender height

Cap height (the height of capital letters), and ascender height (the height of ascenders), are sometimes equal although in certain typefaces they do vary slightly, and the ascender height is marginally higher as demonstrated above.

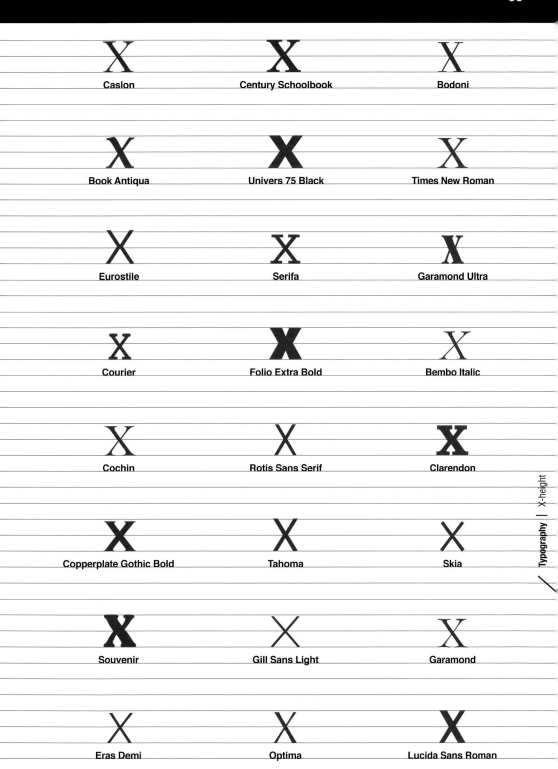

Caslon	Century Schoolbook	Bodoni
Book Antiqua	Univers 75 Black	Times New Roman
Eurostile	Serifa	Garamond Ultra
Courier	Folio Extra Bold	Bembo Italic
Cochin	Rotis Sans Serif	Clarendon
Copperplate Gothic Bold	Tahoma	Skia
Souvenir	Gill Sans Light	Garamond
Eras Demi	Optima	Lucida Sans Roman

Typography | X-height

Absolute measurements

The white lines below are set 12pts apart and form a grid that has an absolute measurement of 60pts. You will notice that the 60pt type sits within these lines rather than being equal to the measurement.

60 point

The point system

The point measurement system was developed in the 19th century by Pierre Fournier and François Didot. The British / American point is 1/72 of an inch.

Type point size

The point size is measured from the ascent line (top of a capital), to the descent line (bottom-most descender). The point system was created for metal type and when cast, type blocks or slugs had a space or shoulder to provide spacing between lines when set. The point size of a font is the measure of the slug not the letter formed on it.

Relative measurements

Some typographical measurements are relative to the point size of the type set. An em set in 60pt type is 60pts. An en is equal to half an em. These two measurements are used to set dashes, fractions and spacing. As the measurement is linked to the type, as the type enlarges, so does the element.

M   M

Ems, Ens and Hyphens

Em

An em is a unit of measurement derived from the width of a square body of the cast upper case 'M'. An em equals the size of a given type, i.e. the em of 60pt type is 60 points. It is used for paragraph indents and denoting nested clauses.

En

An en is a unit of measurement equal to half of one em. It is used in Europe to denote nested clauses. It can also be used to mean 'to' in phrases such as, chapters 10–11, and 1975–1981. An en rule is also used to mean 'and', for example, between two surnames on the spine of a book.

Hyphen

A hyphen is typically one-third the length of an em. It is used to separate parts of compound words, to link the words of a phrase in adjectival hyphenation and to connect the syllables of a word that is split between separate lines.

Client: Diesel
Design: KesselsKrammer
Typographic summary:
Pattern created using a
wide variety of point sizes

Diesel

A variety of point sizes is used to create this poster for a Diesel campaign.
The resulting pattern of typesizes conveys a sense of natural harmony. The fixed
measure and varying typesizes create a dense block of type, instilling different
textures and patterns in the design and giving the larger type the appearance of
pull-quotes. This is often referred to as typographic color, a term that relates to
the relative tonal values of typography.

Client: Christina Zurfluh
Design: Designbolaget
Typographic summary:
Long em rules and quotation
marks as graphic devices

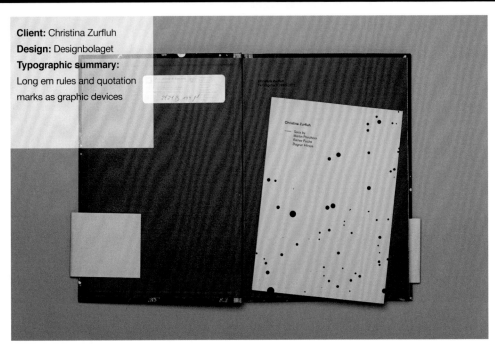

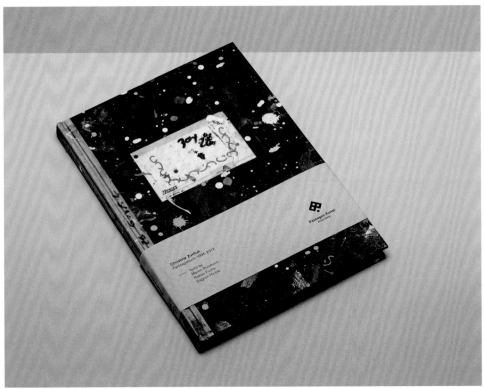

ch zugic
nicht nur in
de wird im
chensysteme
erdeutlichen,
harakter ist auc
erfläche ohnehin an
dazugehö-

sein,
in solches „Ge
z abgesehen davon, da
erte Landschaften mit Höhenso
rte" liefert das Buch, das zur Orientieru
m dabei hilft, die Notizen zu verstehen.

erance:
. von Peter
uttgart 2008,

2 ——
„If the artist carries through his idea
and makes it into visible form, then
all the steps in the process are of
importance. The idea itself, even if not
made visual, is as much a work of art
as any finished product. All intervening
steps—scribbles, sketches, drawings,
failed works, models, studies, thoughts,
conversations—are of interest."
Sol LeWitt, „Paragraphs on Conceptual
Art", in: Artforum, Juni 1967, Bd. 5,
Nr. 10, S. 79–83.

3 ——
Werner Stegmair: „Weltabkürzungs-
kunst: Orientierung durch Zeichen",
in: Zeichen und Interpretation,
hrsg. von Josef Simon, Suhrkamp,
Frankfurt am Main 1994, S. 119–141,
S. 134.

Typography | Absolute and relative measurements

Christina Zurfluh

Pictured is a facsimile of the sketchbook of Swiss artist Christina Zurfluh created
by Designbolaget that features the use of long em rules as a graphic device to
present captions and notes. Also notice how the quotation marks have been set,
with the opening marks set on the baseline. These interventions highlight how the
relatively standard, basic elements of typographic setting can be tweaked with small
details that make a difference to the overall aesthetic effect of the typography and
help differentiate a design.

Industry view: TOKY

Creating wayfinding signage is one of the most challenging areas of design due to its need to communicate succinctly and accurately to a varied audience over time. That challenge is amplified when the client is known for producing innovation.

How is designing type for signage for public places evolving?

The most challenging part of this brand identity was finding the right way to extend the brand into wayfinding signage. MIT students are notorious for hacking systems to create unexpected results, and we were very concerned that any system of prompts from the signage to a visitor's smartphone could be used to launch inappropriate or offensive websites, or even more nefarious invaders. As designers we rather despise the QR code but we tested several options for security, longevity and ease of use, and the QR code had the best scores on all metrics. Creating signage that allows visitors to access complex layers of virtual information – especially visitors who are less technically inclined – is undergoing a rapid evolution, and is one of the most exciting aspects of design in the built environment.

What was the design decision behind the selection of the typeface?

All typography was evaluated for a united presentation in both offline printed materials and online. The typefaces had to have webfont extensions as well as full character sets for use in print media. They also had to convey the contemporary spirit of the List Center, while feeling rooted in a scientific heritage. We landed on Effra because it hit all the right notes, and was not yet overused in the Cambridge/Boston region.

TOKY is a US design agency headquartered in St Louis, Missouri that specializes in branding and creating identities in addition to building complex websites and designing sophisticated publications.

The digital application for the List Visual Arts Center with the same simple, intuitive navigation and color schemes as the signage.

The branding and logo are distinctive and eye-catching, yet it uses quite a blocky sans serif. Why did you chose this over a lighter weight font?

The logo concept requires the words to be read in both horizontal and vertical dimensions. To make that happen, the TOKY designers experimented with many kinds of letterforms, ultimately determining that a blocky, almost square custom-drawn monospace letter worked best. The 'I' and 'T' are split symmetrically, so the letterforms had to be chunky enough for the split to be seen. We tried many versions until we found forms that reflected the contemporary spirit of the List Center at MIT.

How did you arrive at the concept of the logo that combines MIT and LIST? It feels solid and creates a bridge between them. Was this the intention?

Yes, precisely. The List Center is integral to the MIT campus, and sits at a major crossroads. This is reflected in the logo. MIT entities also have a history of using the MIT letterforms in experimental and playful ways, and we tried hard to find forms that had not already been done.

Industry view | TOKY

Client: Absolut Label
Design: KesselsKramer
Typographic summary:
Eclectic collection of
typefaces in harmony
with their subject matter

Type classification

The myriad typefaces available makes a classification system essential. Typefaces can be classified according to their inherent characteristics, but in order to understand how typefaces are classified, one must be familiar with the terminology used to describe the different elements that form a character. As we discussed many typefaces originate in designs that were originally cast in metal or date from the work of stonemasons. Even in the digital age, typefaces still contain the distinct elements associated with the physical necessities of the moment in which they were created.

Typeface classification is based on anatomic characteristics and there are four basic type categories: Roman, gothic, script and block (*Human Factors in Engineering Design*, Sanders & McCormick, 1993). These are further sub-classified: Roman houses all serif typefaces; gothic contains sans serif typefaces; script contains typefaces that mimic handwriting; and block (or blackletter) contains typefaces based on German manuscript handwriting. An additional category, 'graphic' (or 'experimental' or 'symbol'), includes typefaces that do not naturally fit into any of the four sub-categories.

Display type is a visual voice. Without reading it imparts its message. Laura Worthington

Absolut Label

These spreads are from the first issue of the Absolut-sponsored fashion magazine. Designed by KesselsKramer, they feature distinctive typefaces for the covers to reflect the varied locations covered in the publication. The covers pictured feature a stencil typeface; a retro-futuristic, graphic typeface; a geometric typeface with exaggerated descenders; a gothic, italic, bold typeface; an extra-light display type with a distinctive dot on the 'i'; a serif typeface; hand drawn type with script and a typewriter style typeface used almost as an anti-fashion statement.

𝕭lock

Block, blackletter, gothic, old English, black or broken typefaces are based on the ornate writing style prevalent during the Middle Ages. Nowadays, fonts such as Fette Faktur (above) seem heavy, antiquated and difficult to read in large text blocks.

Roman

Roman types, such as Garamond (above) have proportionally spaced letters and serifs, and were originally derived from Roman stone inscriptions. It is the most readable type and is commonly used for body text.

Gothic

Gothic, sans serif or lineale typefaces such as Grotesque MT (above) do not have the decorative touches that typify roman typefaces. Their clean and simple design makes them ideal for display text, but may make them difficult to read in long passages.

Script

Script typefaces such as Kuenstler Script (above) are designed to imitate handwriting so that when printed the characters appear to be joined up. As with human handwriting, some are easier to read than others.

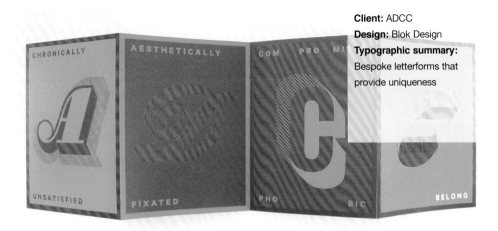

Client: ADCC
Design: Blok Design
Typographic summary:
Bespoke letterforms that provide uniqueness

ADCC

While most typefaces can be described by the main type classification systems there is a wide range of eclectic and characterful typefaces that can lend a sense of playfulness and identity to a design, such as these characters created by Blok Design for the Advertising and Design Club of Canada. Many such characters are one-offs, that is, they are created as single characters rather than as part of a whole font, and highlight the design-focused nature of the organization.

Block typefaces

Block, blackletter, broken, old English or gothic typefaces (not to be confused with sans serif gothic), are based on the heavy, ornate writing style that was prevalent during the Middle Ages. Due to the complexity of the letterforms they can be hard to read – particularly if used in large blocks of text – and therefore usually serve a similar function as the use of scripts or initial capitals. Legibility is however linked to familiarity, thus the gothic sans serif styles that are common today would be equally hard to decipher for someone in the Middle Ages.

Goudy Text

ABCDEFGHIJKLMNOPQRSTUVWXYZ
abcdefghijklmnopqrstuvwxyz 1234567890

Engravers Old English

ABCDEFGHIJKLMNOPQRSTUVWXYZ
abcdefghijklmnopqrstuvwxyz 1234567890

This text is set in Goudy Text, which was designed by Morris Fuller Benton and Joseph W Phinney in 1904. As you can see, when a sizeable amount of text is set in a block typeface the ornate letters affect legibility. This has more to do with the text styles that we, as readers, are accustomed to interpreting than being a fault of such typefaces. When printing was in its formative years those people who could read would have had little trouble reading this text, but as we are now accustomed to reading simpler, cleaner typefaces, the decorative elements of block confuse the eye and slow down tracking from letter to letter. Legibility can be improved by being more generous with the tracking between letters or the space between words.

Typography | Block typefaces

Roman typefaces

The decorative serifs of roman typefaces help the eye track from letter to letter, which is why they are most typically used for body text. Roman typefaces comprise the oldest typeface classification and its origins were founded in text that was carved into Roman stonework.

Many variations of roman typefaces have been developed. These variations can be further sub-classified as Old Style Venetian (or Humanist), Old Style Aldine (or Garaldes), Old Style Dutch, Old Style Revival, Transitional, Didone, Slab serif (or Egyptian), Clarendon, and Glyphic.

Examples of roman typefaces
Cochin and Souvenir are both serif typefaces but they are quite different. In particular take note of the 'Q', 'g', 'J' and 'K' characters. Looking at such characters is a key way to distinguish between different typefaces, for example does the 'Q' have a tail or is it crossed; is the 'g' double-storey or does it have a tail?

Cochin

ABCDEFGHIJKLMNOPQRSTUVWXYZ
abcdefghijklmnopqrstuvwxyz 1234567890

Souvenir

ABCDEFGHIJKLMNOPQRSTUVWXYZ
abcdefghijklmnopqrstuvwxyz 1234567890

Client: Deutsche Bank
Design: Spin
Typographic summary:
Cooper Black typeface combined with hand-drawn imitation. Heavily bracketed slur serif (see page 54)

(see page 54)

Typography | Roman typefaces

Up and Down / Back and Forth

This catalog for works by artist Richard Artschwager was created by Spin design studio and features a series of charcoal-on-paper drawings. The inner pages of the book are reflected in the design of the outer. The outer uses Cooper Black – an extra bold old style revival typeface – set in pink against a woodgrain background. Cooper Black is also used for captions inside the publication. The inner features a reproduction of the cover hand-drawn in charcoal, which is a prelude to the work that follows.

Perhaps it is because the roman typefaces are such an important mainstay of the printed word that so many variations have been developed. Over time, roman typefaces have been modified to reflect changes in style, which has resulted in the evolution of new sub-classifications. These sub-classifications help us to more precisely define and distinguish serif typefaces, as the differences between them can be extremely subtle and therefore hard to spot. Some typefaces straddle two or more classification groups to further complicate matters. Remember though the classifications exist as a guide and not a restriction when specifying a job.

Old style

Old style (or Antiqua) typefaces were developed in the 16th and 17th centuries to replace block typefaces as standard letterforms in use. Distinguished by their irregularity and slanted ascender serifs with low contrast between the thick and thin strokes. They also possess bracketed serifs and a left-inclined stress.

ABCDEFGHIJKLMNOPQRSTUVWXYZ
abcdefghijklmnopqrstuvwxyz 1234567890

Bembo

Bembo was created by Monotype in 1929 for a Stanley Morison project. It is based on a roman-face cut by Francesco Griffo da Bologna, which Aldus Manutius used to print Pietro Bembo's 1496 publication of *De Aetna*. Morison modified letterforms such as the 'G' to create a typeface with legibility that was suitable for almost any application.

Transitional

Transitional typefaces have a medium contrast between their thick and thin strokes with a lower degree of left-inclined stress. A distinguishing feature of a transitional typeface is a flat, or triangular tip where the diagonal strokes meet, as can be seen in the 'W'.

ABCDEFGHIJKLMNOPQRSTUVWXYZ
abcdefghijklmnopqrstuvwxyz 1234567890

Baskerville

The typeface was designed in the 18th century by John Baskerville, a printer from Birmingham, England. A versatile font, Baskerville is used for both body text and display type. Note the absence of a middle serif on the 'W' and the distinctive capital 'Q'.

Client:
The Cursing Stone Project
Design: Why Not Associates
and Gordon Young
Typographic summary:
Set in Bembo, sandblasted
into rock

Typography | Roman variations

The Cursing Stone

The Cursing Stone, created for Glasgow's millennium project, was the result of a collaboration between Why Not Associates and artist Gordon Young. Text quotations from the 1525 *Mother of all Curses* speech by Glaswegian Archbishop Gavin Dunbar were set in Bembo and sandblasted into a 14-ton boulder.

Modern (Classicist or Empire)

These typefaces were developed towards the end of the 18th century and are recognizable by the high-stroke contrast between the thick and thin strokes and the flat unbracketed, often very thin serifs.

ABCDEFGHIJKLMNOPQRSTUVWXYZ
abcdefghijklmnopqrstuvwxyz 1234567890

Bodoni

Based on an 18th-century design by Giambattista Bodoni this typeface has hairline serifs and heavy downstrokes.

Slab serif (or Egyptian)

Slab serif typefaces are distinguished by larger, square serifs, which were considered to be bolder than those of their predecessors. Slab serif typefaces can be further classified into Clarendon and typewriter styles.

ABCDEFGHIJKLMNOPQRSTUVWXYZ
abcdefghijklmnopqrstuvwxyz 1234567890

Serifa

Designed by Adrian Frutiger in 1968, Serifa has a solid appearance and simple slab serifs that do not dominate.

Clarendon

A slab serif sub-classification, which uses subtle serif brackets.

ABCDEFGHIJKLMNOPQRSTUVWXYZ
abcdefghijklmnopqrstuvwxyz 1234567890

Century Schoolbook

Has a greater contrast between the thick and thin strokes than those of slab serif typefaces, that is particularly noticeable on the serifs. The tail of the 'Q' penetrates the counter and the 'J' has a prominent tail dot.

Typewriter

A slab serif sub-classification, which has serifs of equal width to the stem of the character.

ABCDEFGHIJKLMNOPQRSTUVWXYZ
abcdefghijklmnopqrstuvwxyz 1234567890

American Typewriter

This font has additional finials, reminiscent of ink-traps that appear in non-digitized typewriter typefaces.

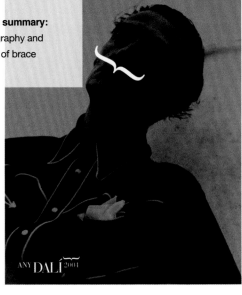

Client: Fundacío
Gala-Salvador Dalí
Design: Bis
Typographic summary:
Bodoni typography and
inventive use of brace

Dalí

Spanish design studio
Bis was asked to
develop an identity to
mark the celebrations
of the 100th anniversary
of Salvador Dalí's birth.
Photographs of the
surrealist painter were
used as the central
iconic image in the
various pieces of work
with typography in
Bodoni; Dalí's favorite
typeface. A brace (curly
bracket) was inserted
over Dalí's face in each
photograph as a clever
imitation of his famous
moustache.

Typography | Roman variations

Many more ornate and noticeable serif styles have developed and are loosely grouped within the following classifications.

SLUR SERIF

Cooper Black – designed by Oswald B Cooper in 1921, this typeface was ahead of its time.
Slur serifs are rounded, almost 'inflated' variations; although ill-defined these serifs are highly distinctive.

BRACKETED SERIF

Garamond – Jean Jannon produced a specimen of typefaces similar to those of Claude Garamond in 1621.
Re-discovered in 1825 and wrongly attributed to Garamond until its true origin was revealed in 1927.

UNBRACKETED SERIF

Memphis – Geometric typeface designed by Rudolf Wolf.
Unbracketed serif typefaces have equal, or monoline, serif and stroke widths.

BRACKETED SLAB SERIF

Clarendon – confusingly both a typeface (see page 52) and a font.
Bracketed slab serifs have monoline serifs 'softened' by joining blends.

UNBRACKETED SLAB SERIF

Rockwell – Produced in the early 20th Century and was issued as Litho Antique.
Unbracketed slab serifs carry the heaviest serifs with no joining blends.

WEDGE SERIF

Meridien – Adrian Frutiger's font, specifically designed to contain no straight strokes.
Wedge serifs display a triangular serif shape.

HAIRLINE SERIF

Bodoni – Morris Fuller Benton's cutting of Giambattista Bodoni's masterpiece typeface.
Hairline serifs have disproportionally thin serifs, but often retain decorative tails, terminals and ears.

Peter Blake Invitation

The typography on this exhibition invitation is developed from found objects belonging to Peter Blake – some of which appeared on his album sleeve design for the Paul Weller's 'Stanley Road'. As the title suggests, the exhibition is about the commercial art practice of Blake. The pronounced wedge-shaped serifs make a distinctive design statement.

Client: London Institute Gallery
Design: Webb & Webb
Typographic summary: Found typographical objects and typeface with distinctive wedge serifs

Typography | Types of serifs

Gothic typefaces

Gothic typefaces, also called sans serif typefaces, have been in existence for more than 100 years. The absence of any serifs, while providing a clean letterform, can impinge on the legibility of the body text.

Historically typographers have tried to address this issue by cutting gothic typefaces suitable for setting body text. Even so gothic typefaces remain limited in their use and are more commonly seen in short bursts as headings and other display functions. Gothic typefaces always have a 'g' with a tail rather than the double-storey 'g' used in some serif typefaces.

Examples of gothic typefaces
Folio and Frutiger illustrate the variety of stroke weights and openness that sans serif typefaces possess. Folio is much bolder in appearance while Frutiger has rounder letterforms. The diversity of gothic fonts means that there are examples that also are lighter and more condensed.

Folio

ABCDEFGHIJKLMNOPQRSTUVWXYZ
abcdefghijklmnopqrstuvwxyz 1234567890

Frutiger

ABCDEFGHIJKLMNOPQRSTUVWXYZ
abcdefghijklmnopqrstuvwxyz 1234567890

Client: Still Waters Run Deep
Design: Still Waters Run Deep
Typographic summary: Metallic printed Helvetica Neue 25, large point size

Still Waters Run Deep

This brochure was produced for the tenth birthday of design studio Still Waters Run Deep. The use of Helvetica Neue 25, demonstrates the simple beauty of lower case typographic detailing such as the terminal tail stroke on the 'a'. This typography is deceptively simple. As the letters used are set in a large point size, the tracking and the kerning (see pages 114 – 121), are far more important than when text is used in a smaller point size (body text for example).

Gothic (or sans serif) typefaces were developed later than their roman counterparts, and within this classification typographers have created an imaginative and widely different body of typefaces. Consequently, a variety of sub-categories have evolved to more precisely define them.

Distinctions between different gothic typefaces can be quite subtle and hard to discern but they can often be seen in a handful of specific characters. The example below shows a clear difference between the double-storey 'g' of Grotesque and the single storey 'g' of Neo-grotesque. Other letters that often show clear distinctions are 'a', 'e', 'M', 'R', and 'y'.

Grotesque

Grotesque typefaces have a more condensed form than those of Neo Grotesques and possess a 'g' with a double-storey, rather than a loop, and a 'G' with a chin.

ABCDEFGHIJKLMNOPQRSTUVWXYZ
abcdefghijklmnopqrstuvwxyz 1234567890

Alternate Gothic No. 2

Alternate Gothic No. 2 has a condensed character body.

Neo-grotesque

Neo-grotesque typefaces have broader characters than those of Grotesques and possess a 'g' with a loop, rather than a double-storey, and a 'G' with a chin.

ABCDEFGHIJKLMNOPQRSTUVWXYZ
abcdefghijklmnopqrstuvwxyz 1234567890

Folio

A sans serif typeface designed by Konrad Bauer and Walter Baum.

Client: The Moving Picture
Company
Design: Form Design
Typographic summary:
White, foil blocked Akzidenz
Grotesk type on white
high-gloss card

The Moving Picture Company

This design, created by Form Design for the Moving Picture Company, uses a
white foil (see page 174) on a high-gloss white board. This adds a tactile element
to the design and also produces a subtle white-on-white effect as the letters
appear when the viewing angle and reflected light change. The text in this example
is set in Akzidenz Grotesk and clearly displays the main characteristics of the
Neo-grotesque classification.

Geometric

Geometric is a descriptive term applied to certain gothic typefaces and also some graphic typefaces (see page 66). The geometric gothic variations have a very rounded shape and are distinguishable by their splayed 'M', 'N', 'V' and 'W' characters. The leg of the 'R' joins the bowl near the stem and the 'G' is chinless.

ABCDEFGHIJKLMNOPQRSTUVWXYZ
abcdefghijklmnopqrstuvwxyz 1234567890

Futura BQ
Futura BQ demonstrates the splayed 'M', 'N', 'V' and 'W', the leg of the 'R' joining the loop near the stem and the chinless 'G'.

Humanist

Humanist typefaces are similar to geometric ones as they also possess splayed 'M', 'N', 'V' and 'W', a chinless 'G' and an 'R' with a leg joining the bowl near the stem. However, they have more stroke weight contrast and a double-storey 'g'.

ABCDEFGHIJKLMNOPQRSTUVWXYZ
abcdefghijklmnopqrstuvwxyz 1234567890

Optima
Optima has the double-storey 'g' and shows the contrast between the weights of higher strokes.

Square

Square typefaces, as the name suggests, have squared characters rather than rounded characters. The 'g' has a tail and the 'Q' has a tail that crosses the bowl. The 'G' is chinless.

ABCDEFGHIJKLMNOPQRSTUVWXYZ
abcdefghijklmnopqrstuvwxyz 1234567890

Eurostile
Eurostile clearly has a squarer appearance when compared to the other typefaces on this spread.

Client: Yauatcha
Design: North
Typographic summary:
Tightly tracked Futura SB
extra light

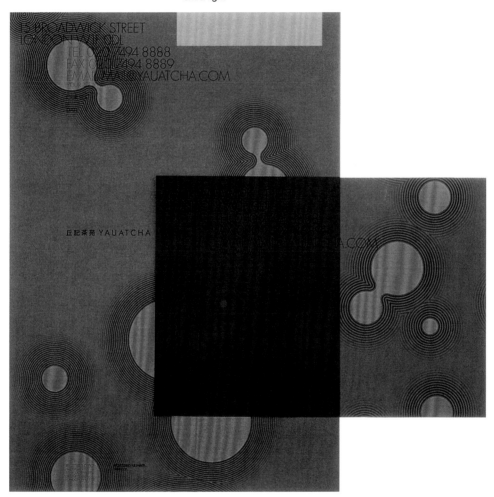

Yauatcha

This stationery for Yautacha by North design studio uses Futura SB extra light, tightly tracked to give a very elegant and controlled appearance. The stationery uses bold, abstracted patterns of tea plant growth on the reverse that show through the page. The fluorescent circular pattern on the reverse invokes the impression of liquid and contrast with the serene nature of the typography.

Rounded variations possess rounded rather than squared-off stroke endings, which result in slightly more relaxed and visually appealing letterforms. Many of these rounded variations find their origins in other typefaces (e.g. Helvetica Rounded is based on standard Helvetica). The rounding of these established typefaces creates a more open, spacious and less condensed appearance.

ABCDEFGHIJKLMNOPQRSTUVWXYZ
abcdefghijklmnopqrstuvwxyz 1234567890
ABCDEFGHIJKLMNOPQRSTUVWXYZ
abcdefghijklmnopqrstuvwxyz 1234567890

Helvetica Rounded

Rounded version of Max Miedinger's classic design, Haas Grotesk; later named Helvetica (an adaptation of the the Latin name for Switzerland 'Helvetia'). The rounded variation is a direct adaptation of the original sans serif (shown top in black).

ABCDEFGHIJKLMNOPQRSTUVWXYZ
abcdefghijklmnopqrstuvwxyz 1234567890

Vag Rounded

Designed by Adrian Williams for Volkswagen in 1979, Vag Rounded exhibits similar characteristics to Helvetica Rounded but there are noticeable differences. The letter 'a' is noticeably geometric and the lowercase 'j' and 'y' are rendered without the curved stroke at the end. The vertical stems of the uppercase 'M' are noticeably oblique.

ABCDEFGHIJKLMNOPQRSTUVWXYZ
abcdefghijklmnopqrstuvwxyz 1234567890

Arial Rounded Bold

Rounded version of Arial, with curved stroke ends like Helvetica Rounded, but with a chinless 'G' as found in Vag Rounded.

Client: RIBA, Arts Council
for England, Habitat
Design: Gavin Ambrose
Typographic summary:
Vag Rounded lower case
used to reflect friendliness
and homeliness

bringing architecture home

what an architect can do for you...

Typography | Rounded variations

Bringing Architecture Home

This concise guide for homeowners about the advantages of hiring an architect was a free cover mount designed for *Elle Decoration* magazine. Vag Rounded was selected as the typeface because its soft edges are friendly and homely, and reflect the nature of the brochure. This makes hiring an architect seem less intimidating.

Script typefaces

Script typefaces were created to mimic handwriting such as that of writing masters from the 17th century. Many have extended termination strokes so that they link together, much like the handwriting they are intended to resemble. They are classified as neither roman nor gothic, as they may share attributes of each.

As script typefaces are difficult to read in large text blocks, their usage is usually confined to providing supplementary decorative details such as brand names or captions.

ABCDEFGHIJKLMNOPQRSTUVWXYZ

abcdefghijklmnopqrstuvwxyz 1234567890

Künstler Script
Künstler Script has its roots in the 19th century lithographic movement and is based on English copperplate scripts and looks quite mechanical.

ABCDEFGHIJKLMNOP2RSTUVWXYZ

abcdefghijklmnopqrstuvwxyz 1234567890

Brush Script
Brush Script was designed by Robert Smith for American Type Founders in 1942 and emulates the look of letters handwritten with an ink brush. The lowercase letters are deliberately irregular to deepen the handwritten text feel.

Kew

For the Kew branding,
SEA Design chose to
interpret the brand name
in script. The typeface
is soft, feminine, personal
and friendly and is
complemented by
atmospheric photography
by Richard Learoyd.

Client: Kew
Design: SEA Design
Typographic summary:
Hand-drawn script which
creates a feminine and
personal feel

Typography | Script typefaces

Graphic typefaces

Graphic typefaces contain characters that could be considered images in their own right. These experimental variations include the widest array of styles with varying degrees of legibility.

Often they may be designed for specific, themed purposes. Characters may absorb the attributes of whatever they are being used to communicate, or they may provide an image connection to the subject matter.

Graphic typefaces can emphasize the drama of a design, although their complexity can adversely affect legibility and are unsuitable for use in body text.

ABCDEFGHIJKLMNOPQRSTUVWXYZ 1234567890

Ironwood
Designed by Joe Redick in 1990 as an homage to the 19th century style woodtypes that were used on 'Wanted' posters in Western films.

ABCDEFGHIJKLMNOPQRSTUVWXYZ
abcdefghijklmnopqrstuvwxyz 1234567890

OCR-A
Created by the American Type Founders in 1968 in the early days of computer optical character recognition technology. The characters were designed so they could easily be read by a machine, even though this makes it more difficult for a human to read. The typeface exaggerated the differences between similar characters such as the 'B' and '8', and '1' and 'I' for example.

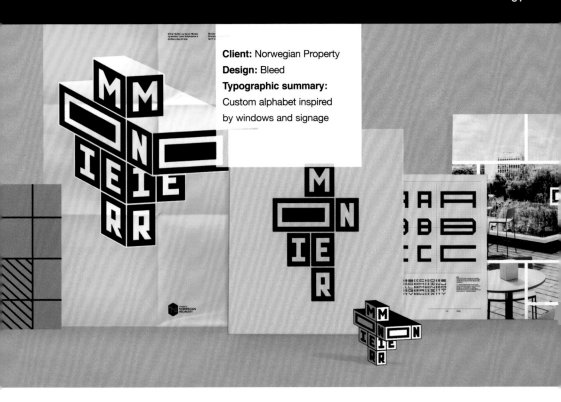

Client: Norwegian Property
Design: Bleed
Typographic summary:
Custom alphabet inspired
by windows and signage

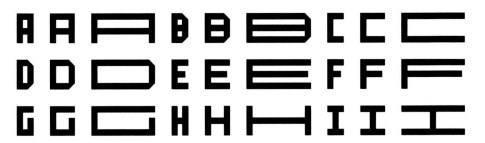

Monier

Monier is a new office building owned by Norwegian Property that has a visual identity created by Bleed that is based on its architecture, which is cubistic and solid. The logotype features a custom graphic typeface that is derived from the building's different window shapes that was part of the original signage on the construction site. The resulting alphabet was redrawn in three different widths to mimic Monier's three-shaped window concept. The dynamic use of the logo, both in terms of transparency and flexible letter elements, gives the design another dimension, rarely seen in property development projects, and helped the building stand out.

Type classification for a digital age

Typefaces created for digital applications fit within the traditional typeface classification model, though they are designed for the constraints of digital applications and, with typically shorter messaging, to be read quickly.

How is typography changing and evolving in the digital age? Type designers are responding to the challenges of the digital age as they have done throughout history when presented with technological change, thus continuing a tradition that can be traced back to Roman carvings in stone monuments. They are also responding to the challenges and opportunities of the technologies with which the type has to be used. During the decades of predominance of lithographic printing, types were designed with elements such as ink traps and thicker serifs, such as slab serifs, so that important detail would not be lost during production and characters did not infill or become saturated by ink.

Ink is no longer a concern in the digital world for type designers but the pixel and resolution are. This means type has to be designed to minimize blockiness or loss of detail when viewed on screen and thus not interfere with legibility and readability.

Zhuck

Pictured is Zhuck (жук) a brand identity created by NB: Studio for an app developed for Russian bank Bank24.ru that caters to disillusioned entrepreneurs, managers and investors who want closer control of their business without getting slowed by the bureaucratic Russian banking system. The brand identity had to work both on and off-line and sees the bookish elegance and seriousness of a serif typeface set in a simple, clean layout offset with touches of color and the Zhuck character to 'appify' standard banking information. Zhuck translates as beetle, which in Russia can mean savvy, clever, entrepreneurial and driven and the Zhuck character cajoles users into action to make doing nothing seem like the difficult option.

Client: Bank24.ru
Design: NB: Studio
Typographic summary:
A serif typeface conveys
seriousness offset by app
features

2 из 5

На счет поступило
145,768₽ рублей от
ООО Владивосток.

На 4 дня позже, но кто
считает? (Жук считает.
Жук всегда все считает.)

Недавно...

Industry view: Urban Influence

Urban Influence is a Pacific Northwest design agency that focuses on details as it aims to demonstrate the life and unique characteristics of the clients it helps rebrand.

What makes the urban environment such a rich source of inspiration for your work?
The building (Pike Building) itself is an inspiration. It was built in 1912 for Pierce Arrow Motor Car Company and used as the showroom until 1921. Over the next three decades it served the Oldsmobile, Nash and Northwest Hudson Motor companies, which is a bit of really amazing history. The service elevator is large enough to put a car in and probably did. During the late 1960s it became REI's headquarters, so that is also pretty cool. The interior space is really expansive and open, so there is so much going on all the time. Our founder built out the space with custom wood desks and incorporated salvaged reclaimed wood from Friday Harbor here in the Northwest. There is so much room that we've been able to customize the walls and extend the Urban Influence brand into the space with a giant golden pigeon and 'future' wall. Finally, there are speakers hardwired into the rafters, which allows us to crank up the music and really get into a nice 'rhythm'.

When you are creating a brand image, what is the role of a typeface? What must it contribute to the brand?
The typeface plays a most important role in creating a brand. It helps evoke a company's foundation and play up emotions subconsciously. Type helps bring it all together and really extend a brand's story.

The original sans serif logo on the Sheridan Hotel was reworked into a bespoke display face.

Typefaces that one can find in the urban environment often hark back to a previous era, whether that is the Victorian age or the 1970s. What is it about this historical referencing that you find appealing?

Well, I believe it was the culture video we worked on crafting in the past that influenced our love for the older typefaces here. They just spoke to us while working in the studio and it really feels like the best choice. I love the history of older type and love seeing the process behind the creation of those faces. Everything was done by hand and a lot of love was put into their craft.

What are the main interventions that you have to make to a typeface that you have found on a sign or the side of a building suitable for a brand that will be used across various media?

A high quality picture is important to have, or something that we can use to lovingly retrace it digitally. If we can't find one, we'll use our best judgment and fill in the gaps. We really try and keep it as close to the original as possible.

For a young designer, what are the key things to bear in mind when using a found typeface from the urban environment? Is it best to use as is or should they tweak it for the project they have?

We'll do some research and do our best to find out the history of the font type, whether it's completely custom or an actual typeface. Sometimes it's an ode to the original, with slight tweaks to distance it further, but often we'll have the client purchase the typeface we used so we're in the clear.

It helps to be careful though, depending on the piece because some tweaks ultimately hurt the original intent of the typeface. There is so much thought and love that went into the originals and we just can't throw that all out the window – let the experts do their thing, you know?

Urban Influence is a Seattle-based design agency with traditional and digital disciplines that specializes in brand development and strategy, graphic design and web design.

Pictured are print elements from a rebrand of Wood Shed Production, a custom craft furniture company in the Pacific Northwest, that capture the craft materials and affable tone of Wood Shed in an organic logo and color palette, designed with simplicity in mind. The brand focuses on the skill and product of the craftsmen while providing a visually enticing means of online access to the company and product.

Industry view | Urban Influence

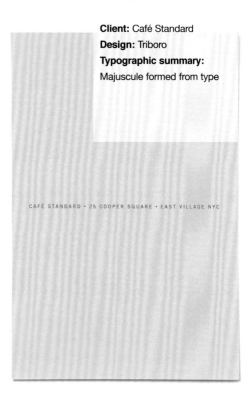

Client: Café Standard
Design: Triboro
Typographic summary:
Majuscule formed from type

CAFÉ STANDARD · 25 COOPER SQUARE · EAST VILLAGE NYC

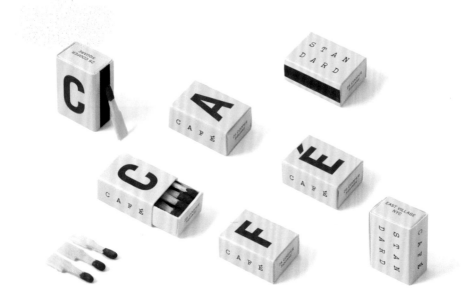

Chapter 3

Choosing type

Typefaces differ one from another; sometimes subtly, sometimes not. The diversity of typeface designs is a testament to their versatility and the range of different functions that they can perform. Typefaces are not created equal as some can be generalists that are useful in many situations while others are specialist tools that are suitable in a more narrow range of applications.

Some typefaces are made to excel in body text in documents while others are made to be displayed at large sizes and read from a distance. Typeface selection is driven by a number of practical factors such as the conditions under which text will be read and the materials it will be produced in, as much as by aesthetic considerations. Poor typeface selection can detract from a design and, at its worst, make text difficult or uncomfortable to read.

The following pages look at the peculiarities and limitations of some typefaces, and their characteristics and relationships to type families. Learning about type characteristics provides insight about how they can best be used and the most appropriate typefaces for any given job.

Typography is two-dimensional architecture, based on experience and imagination, and guided by rules and readability. Hermann Zapf

Café Standard

Pictured is an identity created by Triboro for Café Standard, a café at The Standard East Village that features a three-dimensional majuscule 'S' formed from type that creates a home-made feel.

Navigating the sea of type

There are thousands of typefaces available for a designer to choose from and more are being created every day. Differentiating between different typefaces in order to choose the correct one(s) for a job requires both knowledge about typefaces and experience using them.

Fortunately, with a plethora of printed materials within easy reach of everyone, in addition to digital sources such as websites and apps, it is easy for new designers to view and deconstruct existing work to see what typefaces were used and how they perform.

To do this effectively, it helps to be equipped with some technical knowledge to be able to give expression to the differences and functions that type performs including type families, hierarchies, ligatures and punctuation, for example. Increasing our knowledge about type enables a designer to make better type selections and from a wider array of typefaces. Despite this, there are still occasions when it is necessary to create a bespoke typeface.

Mull of Kintyre

Pictured are stills from a short video created by Planning Unit for Paul McCartney about the making of his hit single Mull of Kintyre that features the song's lyrics projected onto the walls of McCartney's music studio in solid sans serif majuscules such that they become slogans.

Client: Paul McCartney
Design: Planning Unit
Typographic summary:
Lyrics projected onto the walls
in solid sans serif majuscules

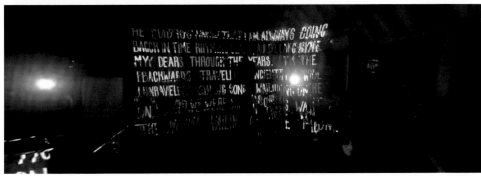

Typography | Navigating the sea of type

Type families

A type family incorporates all the variations of a particular typeface including the range of different weights, widths and italics. These are a useful design tool because they provide the designer with options that work together in a consistent way.

Shown below as an example of the extended type family are some of the many versions of Gill Sans. The variety offered by such a comprehensive typeface is suitable for everything from footnotes to posters, body text to headlines, without the need for any additional typefaces.

ABCDEFGHIJKLMNOPQRSTUVWXYZ
ABCDEFGHIJKLMNOPQRSTUVWXYZ
ABCDEFGHIJKLMNOPQRSTUVWXYZ
ABCDEFGHIJKLMNOPQRSTUVWXYZ
ABCDEFGHIJKLMNOPQRSTUVWXYZ
ABCDEFGHIJKLMNOPQRSTUVWXYZ
ABCDEFGHIJKLMNOPQRSTUVWXYZ
ABCDEFGHIJKLMNOPQRSTUVWXYZ
ABCDEFGHIJKLMNOPQRSTUVWXYZ
ABCDEFGHIJKLMNOPQRSTUVWXYZ
ABCDEFGHIJKLMNOPQRSTUVWXYZ
ABCDEFGHIJKLMNOPQRSTUVWXYZ
ABCDEFGHIJKLMNOPQRSTUVWXYZ

Gill Sans

The above typefaces are from the Gill Sans, sans serif family designed by Eric Gill in the 1920s and based on the typeface used by London Underground. In addition to the many weights and styles, numerals are presented in very different ways for this ever popular typeface. The naming system applied here can appear confusing; it begins with Gill Sans Light, then Gill Sans Light Small Caps, Gill Sans Light Italic and Gill Sans Light Italic Old Style Figures, and continues through the different book weights, the bolds, the blacks, the heavies and the ultras, all with their own small capital and italic variations.

One solution to the confusion of naming type families can be seen clearly if you arrange the weights on a grid, rather than in a column. Here there are four typeface styles: a sans, a semi-sans, a semi-serif and a serif. The sans and the semi sans, more useful in body text situations, carry a wide range of weights. The 'quirkier' semi-serif and serif, more suited to display purposes, carry a reduced variety of weights.

Sans Serif	Semi-sans	Semi-serif	Serif
Rotis Sans Serif Light	Rotis Semi-sans Light		
Rotis Sans Serif Light Italic	*Rotis Semi-sans Light Italic*		
Rotis Sans Serif Regular	Rotis Semi-sans Regular	Rotis Semi-serif Regular	Rotis Serif Regular
Rotis Sans Serif Italic	*Rotis Semi-sans Italic*		*Rotis Serif Italic*
Rotis Sans Serif Bold	**Rotis Semi-sans Bold**	**Rotis Semi-serif Bold**	**Rotis Serif Bold**
Rotis Sans Serif Extra Bold	**Rotis Semi-sans Extra Bold**		

Rotis

Cut in 1989, Rotis is a typeface family that incorporates both serif and sans serif styles in various combinations. It also includes a range of weights or 'colors' such as light, regular, bold and black. Rotis exhibits a current trend for designing typefaces that are available in both serif and sans serif varieties, and indeed mixtures of both. These combinations can offer flexibility, and semi-sans in particular offers a font that's easy to read (like a serif) with the more rigid nature of a sans serif.

Stone Sans	**Stone Serif**	**Stone Informal**
STONE SANS REGULAR	STONE SERIF REGULAR	STONE INFORMAL REGULAR
STONE SANS ITALIC	*STONE SERIF ITALIC*	*STONE INFORMAL ITALIC*
STONE SANS SEMI-BOLD	**STONE SERIF SEMI-BOLD**	**STONE INFORMAL SEMI-BOLD**
STONE SANS SEMI-BOLD ITALIC	***STONE SERIF SEMI-BOLD ITALIC***	***STONE INFORMAL SEMI-BOLD ITALIC***
STONE SANS BOLD	**STONE SERIF BOLD**	**STONE INFORMAL BOLD**
STONE SANS BOLD ITALIC	***STONE SERIF BOLD ITALIC***	***STONE INFORMAL BOLD ITALIC***

Stone

Stone is an extended typeface family designed by Sumner Stone that contains serif, sans serif, and informal styles that all have a roman and italic version in three weights: medium, semibold, and bold. The informal typeface contains a mixture of sans serif and serif characteristics.

Typography | Type families

Adrian Frutiger was prominent in the pantheon of typographers due to the classification grid he developed to show the relationships between the different weights and widths of his Univers typeface.

Originally created for the Univers typeface family in 1951 and it was launched in 1957. A key reason for its success was the numbering system Frutiger developed to show the width and weight relationships between the original 21 cuts, known as Frutiger's grid. The first number relates to weight, and the second to width. The system has been adopted by other designers such as Max Miedinger whose Helvetica typeface is shown below.

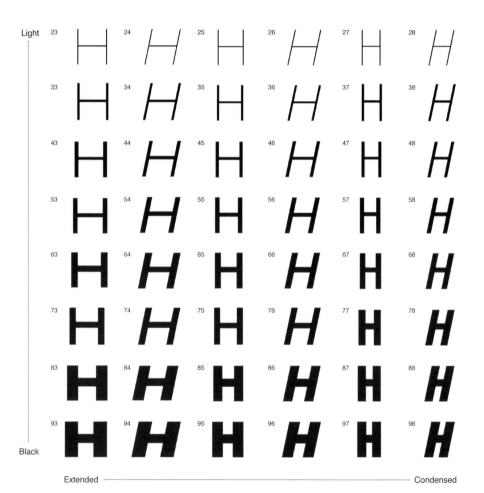

To achieve clarity and a uniform feel many designers restrict themselves to using only two type weights from a particular family, as this is enough to establish a typographic hierarchy without unnecessary elaboration.

Typographical hierarchy

This is usually established using two weights of one typeface. Here the header is set in Helvetica Bold 75 and the body text in Helvetica Roman 55. The difference between the two weights is sufficient for them to be clearly distinguished without the two weights appearing unrelated.

Typographical harmony

This is unattainable if the difference between the two weights is too extreme. Here the solid black appearance of Helvetica Black 95 in the header swallows up the fineness of the Helvetica Ultra Light 25 used in the body text.

Typographical difference

This will pass unnoticed if you use typefaces that are next to each other on the grid. Here the header is set in Helvetica Bold 85 and is accompanied by body text set in Helvetica Bold 75, but the difference between them is barely noticeable.

Typography | Type families

Using multiple typefaces

Although it is possible to complete a design using a single font, it is common for more than this to be used. The use of two or more typefaces immediately presents the opportunity to create a hierarchy, which can greatly ease navigation around a publication.

There are no hard and fast rules concerning which typefaces, or indeed, how many to choose for a design. Certain jobs may require more typographical variety and extreme differences in the type styles used, while in others, the simple addition of a secondary typeface may be used to differentiate footnotes or marginalia from the body text. Below are some general considerations that may prove helpful.

Distinctive typefaces are often used for titles[†]
The body text can then be selected to be used in conjunction with this. Frequently one will be a roman typeface, and the other a gothic[††].

Selected typefaces need to have flexibility[1]

[†]   *Souvenir*
[††] *Helvetica 55*
[1]   *Often a different version of the body copy font will be used for footnotes and marginalia. In this case Helvetica 56.*

Of course this can be reversed[†]
as long as there is a difference between the titling typeface and the body copy[††].

[†]   *Impact*
[††] *Bembo*

If the typefaces are too similar though[†]
The differences between one typeface and another[††] may go unnoticed.

[†]   *Swiss*
[††] *Helvetica Neue*

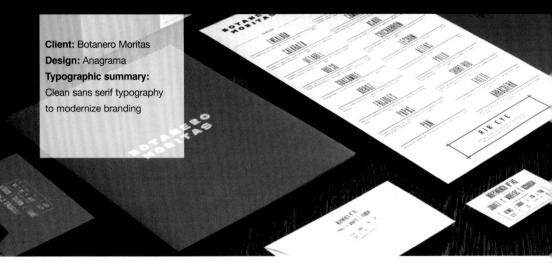

Client: Botanero Moritas
Design: Anagrama
Typographic summary:
Clean sans serif typography
to modernize branding

Botanero Moritas
Pictured are paraphernalia created by Mexican design studio Anagrama for a rebrand of traditional Mexican cantina Botanero Moritas in San Pedro Garza García that features regional cuisine targeted at young adults. The cantina was founded in 1939, making it a distinctive site that is rich in both tradition and history. Rather than take a historical approach, Anagrama provided a revamp that modernized the branding using clean and modern sans serif typography that is a key decorative feature throughout the restaurant space in addition to its usage on printed matter.

Typography | Using multiple typefaces

Text hierarchy

Text hierarchy is a logical and visual guide, which allows the variety of headings that normally accompany body text to be organized. Hierarchy indicates different degrees of importance through the use of point sizes and/or type styles. It is important to note that using an overly complex text hierarchy can be distracting and reduce visual harmony.

A head

The A head is the primary heading usually reserved for the title of a piece. It uses the largest point size (here it is shown in 14pt bold type) to indicate its predominance.

B head

The second hierarchy classification, the B head, has a smaller point size than an A head (here it is shown in 12pt type), but remains larger than that of body text. B heads usually include headings within chapter.

C head

The C head may be the same point size as the body text but could be differentiated by an italic or bold version of the typeface.

Client: The Climate Group
Design: Browns
Typographic summary:
Simple text hierarchy with color differentiation

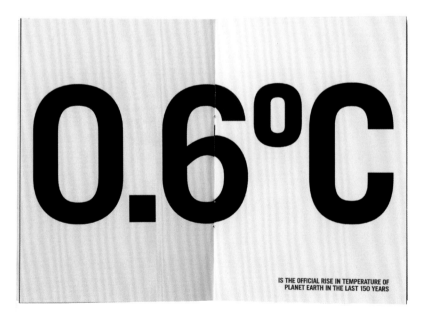

FACT:
THE WORLD IS SET TO WARM BY BETWEEN 1.4 & 5.8°C THIS CENTURY.

BUT THE FUTURE IS NOT YET WRITTEN.

0.6°C

IS THE OFFICIAL RISE IN TEMPERATURE OF PLANET EARTH IN THE LAST 150 YEARS

Typography | Text hierarchy

The Climate Group

Pictured is a brochure created by Browns for an identity for The Climate Group that features easily digestible facts presented with minimal typography and limited color range to focus attention on the climate change message. Elsewhere, headings and body text are set in the same upper case sans serif typeface but differentiated by the use of color.

Text hierarchy for the digital age

Websites and other digital media were often originally built as electronic versions of existing print media using the same hierarchy conventions as the printed form. As digital media matures this is changing and hierarchies appropriate for digital presentation are being adopted and the idea that a webpage is simply an online print page is being left in the past.

While many of the principles remain the same in terms of the spatial relationships, pace and sense of purpose that a hierarchy can instill in a text, they are being tweaked to adapt to changing reading and consuming habits and the particular limitations and possibilities of the viewing devices. Simply changing the typesize for example is not necessarily a good solution for content that is to be used on a smartphone where space is restricted. Similarly, hyperlinks take people straight to the content they are interested in.

Christner Architects

Pictured is a brand rework for the digital space created by TOKY for architectural practice Christner that reinforces the existing brand and features beautiful, full screen images of their work. As web browsers had evolved TOKY rethought how the practice presented itself and its work online with fully responsive content that works on any screen size. While the site makes full use of the graphic capabilities of devices and text use is minimized, it still has a clear hierarchy that is mainly imposed through the use of color, boldface and capitals in one general typeface.

Client: Christner Architects
Design: TOKY
Typographic summary:
Simple text hierarchy for
digital space based on
one general typeface

"We create our most transformative designs when we work in collaboration with organizations that face complex challenges and share our belief in the power of design to address them. By asking good questions and seeking fresh approaches, we deliver environments that realize their full potential, while encouraging the people who enter them to achieve theirs."

John Rexon, AIA
President

OUR HISTORY AND CULTURE

Christner is a
collaborative design firm
bringing innovation,

CHRISTNER

Crafting a collaborative work environment – by design

FULFILLING OUR CLIENTS' VISIONS
THROUGH INSIGHTFUL PLANNING AND
TRANSFORMATIVE DESIGN

TRENDING TOPICS FROM OUR BLOG

Place Attachment: Engendering Loyalty and Love
Presented at SCUP

Planning Process at the University of Chicago Medical
Center Presented at SCUP

CHRISTNER

University of Missouri - St. Louis, College of
Optometry and College of Nursing

VIEW PROJECT

Westminster College, Wallace H. Coulter
Science Center

VIEW PROJECT

CHRISTNER   PRACTICE WORK PEOPLE CULTURE   Q

QUESTION

COLLABORATE

CREATE

Crafting a collaborative work environment – by
design
VIEW PROJECT

Typography | Text hierarchy for the digital age

Type on a page

Type on a page can be styled in a number of different ways; to ease or hinder readability, to convey a certain emotion, to relate to and enhance graphic elements or to create a unique sense of identity and space.

How text is set, and the space within which it is set, can have a dramatic effect on how easy it is to read and on which part of the text grabs the attention of a reader first. This block is quite standard and is set 10pt type on 10pt leading.

Text set 10pt on 10pt.

▓▓This second block includes a 5mm indent, which creates an eye-catching space at the start of a paragraph.

Text set 10pt on 10pt with the inclusion of a 5mm indent.

This third piece uses a space to clearly demarcate a paragraph break.
A space of any size can be inserted (here it is + 2pt), sufficient for it to be noticeable but not exceeding a full line space as with the use of a full return.

Text set 10pt on 10pt with 2mm of space added after the first paragraph.

"With non-hanging punctuation the text appears to shift or be slightly indented, which can be distracting.'

This text block shows non-hanging punctuation such as quotation marks…

"With hanging punctuation the text appears as one single, solid block."

…and how the text block looks using hanging punctuation.

A different point size is not necessary to identify a title.
An emboldened version of a typeface creates sufficient difference to distinguish it from the body text.

This text block uses a hierarchy to distinguish levels of importance.

The grey bars highlight the leading spacing, which is measured from the left-hand margin of the text block to the right-hand margin and, which may or may not be where a line of ranged-left text ends.

In this text block, the 10pt type is set with additional leading (14pt) to open up more space between the lines.

Client: Liberty

Design: Spin

Typographic summary:

Contemporary treatment of

the classic Plantin typeface

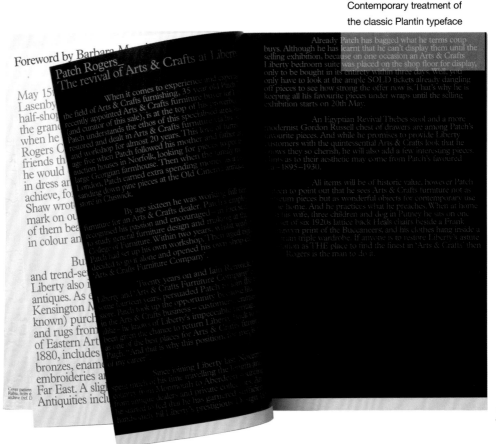

Liberty

This catalog demonstrates that a contemporary feel can be achieved by
using classic typefaces such as Plantin in a modern way. In this example, the
indentation, leading and color all contribute towards producing an elegant, yet
contemporary appearance. Other modern interventions include the use of an
underscore following the author's name and the use of an indent that bites
further into the paragraph than is the accepted norm. Here it is used with more
classical proportions.

Type can be set using a variety of horizontal alignments, as demonstrated below. Alignment, when used effectively, can help harmonize text with other elements in the design, but large text blocks that are not left aligned or justified can become difficult and tiring to read as the eye loses its place.

A right-ranged text block can be difficult to read as the starting place for each line is irregular.

Range right, ragged left

Left-ranged text is commonplace. It is the simplest alignment to read as each line starts on the far left.

Range left, ragged right

Centered type is not commonly used for body text as it also suffers from irregular starting points for each line. It is often used for headings and pull-quotes.

Centered

Justified text creates a neat text block with straight sides. This can introduce unsightly gaps between words as the lines are stretched to fill the measure, as shown in the second line here.

Justified

The gaps in justified blocks of text are easier to identify if you turn the text upside down. This prevents you from reading it and therefore makes the gaps more obvious to the eye.

The gaps in the second line of inverted text stand out more sharply than in the third line of the same text block when viewed the right way up.

The gaps in the second line of inverted text stand out more sharply than in the third line of the same text block when viewed the right way up.

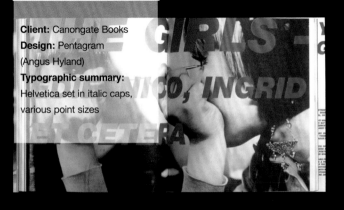

Client: Canongate Books
Design: Pentagram
(Angus Hyland)
Typographic summary:
Helvetica set in italic caps,
various point sizes

Andy Warhol:
The Factory Years

Angus Hyland, partner at Pentagram, produced this design for *Andy Warhol: The Factory Years 1964-67* on behalf of Canongate Books. The volume is a collection of images and reflections by New York photographer Nat Finkelstein, who was the unofficial photographer at the Factory for more than two years.

The text, which describes Finkelstein's recollections and points of note is set in a Helvetica sans serif typeface. This is displayed in italic caps and the point size changes throughout the book to reflect the frenetic nature of the commentary provided.

Numerals

There are two classifications of numerals: Old style (or lower case), and lining (or upper case). Lining numerals are aligned to the baseline and are all of equal height, whereas old style numerals do not, which means they can be difficult to read.

Lining numerals have characters with equal height and monospaced widths so that each numeral occupies exactly the same width as any other. This characteristic can often provide a great deal of addtional display space, which it may be necessary to kern (or remove), particularly after the numeral '1'.

Lining (or upper case) numerals

Numerals, when set as lining figures in body text – 5,452.16 for example – have a tendency to look oversized when compared to their old style counterparts. As the figures are of equal size to capital letters and occupy the same space – from baseline to cap height – they receive too much prominence in body text.

Old style (or lower case) numerals

Old style numerals – 5,452.16 – look in proportion to the lower case characters. The numbers 6 and 8 sit on the baseline and reach the cap height, while 1, 2 and 0 sit on the baseline and align to the x-height.

The remaining characters, 3, 4, 7, and 9 effectively have descenders that help to blend the numerals into body text.

Lining (or upper case) serif numerals

1234567890

Old style (or lower case) serif numerals

1234567890

Although the differences between these styles of numerals may appear subtle, they can alter the overall readability and appearance of numerical data. There are no hard and fast rules to numeral selection, indeed you may be limited due to the nature of the typography used elsewhere.

Sans serif typefaces typically only carry a set of lining numerals, while serif variations will often have both lining and old style numerals. There are exceptions (see below), although certain typefaces may only be available in limited weights.

As a general guide, lining numerals work better in tabular matter as there are no ascenders or descenders to disrupt the flow of the eye. Old style figures are better suited to use within body text as their adjusted size and positioning is in harmony with the proportions of the lower case alphabet.

Lining (or upper case) sans serif numerals

1234567890

Old style (or lower case) sans serif numerals

1234567890

Typesetting is about making choices, and good typesetting is about making the right choices. Even setting a simple column of numerals requires consideration. As with most examples in this book, a successful design rests upon a clear understanding of what the brief is attempting to achieve. These three examples of setting numerals (below), all have unique advantages and are used for specific reasons.

Right alignment
The numerals will right align in the column only if they have an equal number of characters before and after the decimal point. This makes the vertical alignment of characters irregular and greatly impedes legibility.

£12.50
221.73*
124.76
£358.99

Decimal (or character) alignment
Inevitably columns of numerals are irregular. Decimal point (or character) alignment can compensate for this by aligning on the decimal point. However, these numerals aren't monospaced and so the narrow number '1' causes misalignment.

£   12.50
221.73*
124.76
£   358.99

Monospaced numerals
Here, each character and punctuation mark occupies an equal amount of space, and automatically aligns, even the number '1'.

£   12.50
221.73*
124.76
£   358.99

Highlights

EMI Recorded Music
EMI Recorded Music's market share rose 1.6 points to 14.1%.

31 albums sold 1m copies or more.

The Beatles *1* became the fastest selling album ever. It has now sold over 21m units.

Turnover
£2,282.0m

Operating profit
£227.5m

EMI Music Publishing
EMI Music Publishing remains the world's biggest and best music publisher.

Synchronisation revenues increased 11.1%, led by deals as diverse as the James Bond theme for Playstation, and *Singin' in the Rain* for VISA.

Turnover
£390.7m

Operating profit
£105.0m

Client: EMI

Design: SEA Design

Typographic summary:
Mixture of numeral alignments employed to create dynamic layout of financial information

Adjusted diluted earnings per share (pence)

Dividends per share (pence)

Financial Summary

	Year ended 31 March 2001 £m	Year ended 31 March 2000 £m	Change %
Group turnover	2,672.7	2,386.5	12.0
EBITDA (i)	389.5	348.4	11.8
Group operating profit before operating exceptional items and amortisation	332.5	290.6	14.4
Profit before taxation, exceptional items and amortisation (ii)	259.5	245.4	5.7
Adjusted diluted earnings per share (iii)	22.3p	19.2p	16.1
Dividends per share	16.0p	16.0p	-
Return on sales (iv)	12.4%	12.2%	
Interest cover (v)	5.3x	6.9x	

(i) EBITDA is Group operating profit before operating exceptional items, depreciation and amortisation of goodwill and music copyrights.
(ii) Profit before taxation, exceptional items and amortisation is before both operating and non-operating exceptional items and amortisation of goodwill and music copyrights.
(iii) Adjusted diluted earnings per share is before both operating and non-operating exceptional items and amortisation of goodwill and music copyrights.
(iv) Return on sales is defined as Group operating profit before operating exceptional items and amortisation of goodwill and music copyrights as a percentage of turnover.
(v) Interest cover is defined as the number of times Group EBITDA is greater than Group finance charges.

Decimal alignment
These figures are conventionally aligned on the decimal point, allowing additional symbols to be included without breaking the vertical harmony that the figures naturally create.

Left alignment
Here graphic figures align left, and related units are reproduced in a much smaller point size in the copy that sits to the right. Although unconventional, this makes a clear and dynamic layout that emphasizes the value of the figures.

/ **Typography** | Numerals

EMI

Annual reports and financial literature require specific attention to the way in which numerals are set. This annual report for EMI by SEA Design uses a mixture of alignments to create an engaging design focusing on the clear bold use of figures. The cover of this brochure can be seen on page 176.

Drop and standing capitals

A drop capital (or drop cap) is a design feature whereby the initial letter of the first word in a paragraph is set in a larger point size and aligned with the top of the first line of text. The drop cap may be an ornate typeface as in medieval illuminated manuscripts, or something simpler that may have the body text wrapped around it.

D rop caps are eye-catching elements that can dramatically affect the appearance of a text block depending on its point size and the number of text lines it occupies.

 hen using drop caps, the first letter of the body text must be removed so that it is not repeated. Where possible, you should avoid using any word if the first letter is removed, the remaining characters will form a new word – as above where 'When' becomes 'W hen'. Finally, avoid using a drop cap for a word that only has two letters. Theoretically, a drop cap can occupy any number of text lines. However, you should take into account the measure of the block in which it will be placed so that it does not result in an unbalanced or uneven look.

 ot nearly as common as the drop cap, the standing capital is also a typesetting alternative. It sits on the same baseline as the rest of the text, yet without the body text stacking up against it, as is seen with a drop cap. When used, care needs to be taken to ensure that the text is sufficiently kerned so as not to create a typographical distraction.

Client: The Logan Collection
Design: Aufuldish + Warinner
Typographic summary:
Large, green, bracketed
capital, overprinted with
body text

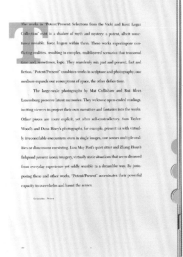

The Logan Collection

This is a catalog published by The Logan Collection of Vail, Colorado, USA to celebrate its tenth anniversary of collecting contemporary art. The catalog features a collection of essays and installation photographs from works in the collection. Aufuldish + Warinner overprinted large, green, bracketed capitals with body text to imitate drop caps and form a focal point on the text pages. Although it is overprinted, the capital still fulfills its function of leading the eye to the start of the text block.

Special characters

Letterforms and numerals alone are not sufficient to structure comprehensive textual information or communicate phonetic stresses and the infinite number of ideas that we wish to convey.

In order to satisfy this function we need various special characters. Punctuation enables us to qualify, quantify and organize information; accents provide us with information about how a letter is stressed or sounds; and pictograms provide shorthand information such as currency units. The following list, while not exhaustive, introduces all the major characters which, if correctly used, can enhance a design.

All typefaces are not equal

Most typefaces contain punctuation and miscellaneous characters but not all carry a comprehensive range of both. Graphic typefaces tend to have fewer special characters and it is worth exploring this before selecting a typeface for a design. Additional characters may not be required for all jobs but for some, a reduced set of special characters could be problematic. A dotless 'i' for example is a special character that can solve specific typographical problems but is not included with all fonts.

Time   Time   Time

Sometimes a typeface will be selected on the grounds of certain characters that it contains, for example, if you wanted a complete set of accentuated small caps and swashes this will limit your typeface choices. Centaur (below) is an exmaple of a typeface that comes with these characters.

!"#$%&'()*+,-./:;<=>?@^_`{|}~¡¢£¤¥¦§¨©ª«¬®¯°±
µ¶·¸¹º»¼½¾¿ÀÁÂÃÄÅÆÇÈÉÊËÌÍÎÏÐÑÒÓÔÕÖ×ØÙÚ
ÛÜÝÞßàáâãäåæçèéêëìíîïðñòóôõö÷øùúûüýþÿıŁŁŒœŠšŸŽžƒ
ABCDEFGHIJKLMNOPQRSTUVWXYZaeflegksprsttvwz

The London Institute Gallery

Client: London Institute Gallery
Design: Webb & Webb
Typographic summary: Inverted exclamation marks used to represent people

MUNICIPAL ART GALLERY AND MUSEUM.
NOTICE

10 November - 19 December 2003

This exhibition is dedicated to my wife Chrissy, my daughters Liberty, Daisy and Rose, my family and friends.
Thanks to Michael Fraser, Ceri House, the London Institute, AB Foundry, Waddington Galleries, Brian Webb and Gavin Turk. PB

THE LONDON
INSTITUTE CAMBERWELL COLLEGE OF ARTS
CENTRAL SAINT MARTINS COLLEGE
OF ART AND DESIGN CHELSEA COLLEGE OF ART
AND DESIGN LONDON COLLEGE OF FASHION
LONDON COLLEGE OF PRINTING

Peter Blake Sculpture 10 November – 19 December 2003. The London Institute Gallery, 65 Davies Street, London W1K 5DA.
Catalogue photographed over two weeks during September 2003 at Peter Blake's Studio and AB Fine Art Foundry, London, by Steven Bull and
Brian Webb. Further photography: p9 left Anon, right Tate Photography / David Clark, p16 & 29 Tate Photography / Marcus Leith and Andrew
Dunkley, p14 Waddington Galleries / Prudence Cuming Associates. Words Encore © Peter Blake, Aside © Gavin Turk, and Peter The Sculptor
© Michael Benson. Exhibition Curators Brian Webb and Peter Blake. Exhibition Design Trickett Associates. Catalogue Design Brian Webb and
Chris Glenster, Webb & Webb Design Limited. Jacket Printed by Hand & Eye Letterpress. Catalogue Printed by Empress Litho.

Typography | Special characters

London Institute Gallery

Webb & Webb designed this guide for an exhibition of sculptor Peter Blake's work, held at the London Institute Gallery. The brochure uses inverted exclamation marks to mirror the shape of Blake's sculptures. The exclamation marks resemble people and reflect individual personalities via the wood-block printing method used. The family of exclamation marks grows on successive pages, initially starting with two members, then increasing to four and so on.

Ligatures

A ligature is a typographical device that joins two or three separate characters together to form a single unit. They are a solution to the interference that certain character combinations create.

The term ligature derives its name from 'Ligare', which is the Latin word for 'bind'. A ligature may also represent a specific sound such as the capital Æ diphthong. Interestingly the ampersand character (&), is a ligature of the word Latin 'et', which means 'and'.

Lower case combinations

The ascender or the 'f' character and the serif belonging to the ascender of the following letter can sometimes look as if they are interfering with each other. Rather than trying to separate them by using kerning, they are often joined by a ligature (as shown below). Similarly, where the dot of the 'i' or 'j' can appear cumbersome when following the 'f', a ligature that joins at the crossbar can be used, and the dot removed.

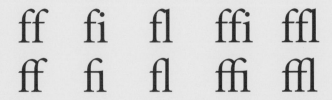

ff fi fl ffi ffl
ff fi fl ffi ffl

Dante /Dante Expert
Pictured above left are the standard characters and, below left, with their replacement ligatures. The 'i' loses its dot and the arms of the 'ff' join in one continuous crossbar.

Upper case combinations

For the same reasons as outlined above, ligatures are also used in pairings of certain capitals.

st Th sp ck Hi
st Th sp ck Hi

Poetica
Designed by Robert Slimbach and modeled on chancery handwriting scripts developed during the Renaissance that were the basis for italic typefaces.

University of Sussex

This prospectus for the University of Sussex, designed by Blast design studio, features a ligature joining the institution's initials and forming part of a new identity for the university.

An amended version of Baskerville was cut for the prospectus and is also used as the header typeface and for campus signage. It has a single terminal on lower case ascenders such as 'h' and a round foot on the 'm' for example. The rounding of the new cut is used as a key component of the university's logo ligature.

Client: University of Sussex
Design: Blast
Typographic summary:
Ligature based logotype and amended Baskerville typeface creating a unifying identity

Typography | Ligatures

The poster pairs the simplified typography with an open, aspirational image within which the central prominence of the ligature suggests inclusivity and connection.

The right character for the job

A typeface contains a suite of supporting punctuation characters that not only serve a grammatical function, but that also add another layer of graphic elements that can add to, enhance or distract from a design.

Typographic quotation marks (curly quotes) and primes

Below left are single and double quotation marks, whilst below right are single and double primes. It is a common mistake to use primes instead of the correct 'curly quotes'. The single prime is used to denote inches, minutes or points. The double prime is used for feet and hours. Knowing the correct character for a job is only half the problem as you also need to understand different usage conventions. Confusingly American and English settings are the opposite of each other. In British English, the primary quotation mark is the single mark, while a quote within this uses double quotation marks.

'Single'   "Double"   'Single'   "Double"

The 'dotless i'

A 'dotless' i is supplied with most typefaces. Although strictly speaking it is not a ligature, it performs a similar function and is used where space can be restricted, as it tucks under an over-hanging character such as the arm of a ' T'.

i   ı   Tight   Tıght

Accents

Most typefaces come with common accents: acute, (á, é, í, ó, ú), grave (à, è, ì, ò, ù), cedilla (ç), umlauts or dieresis (ä, ë, ï, ö, ü), circumflex (â, ê, î, ô, û), ring (å) and tilde (ã). Typefaces often contain accents as individual characters (1) that can be used with letters (2), to create accented characters by kerning them together. Some resulting characters (3) are regularly used in Polish but are unavailable in standard character sets.

Client: Swiss RE CfGD
Design: Frost* Design
Typographic summary:
Quotation marks as icon

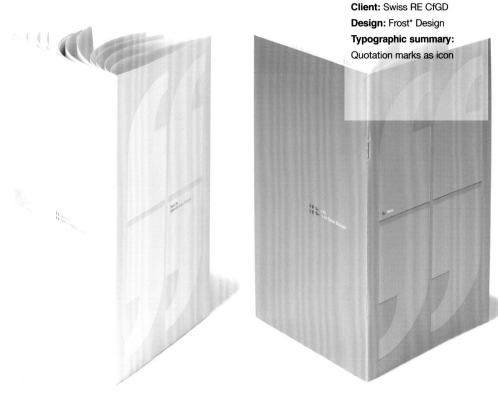

Typography | The right character for the job

Swiss RE CfGD

This identity for reinsurance company Swiss RE's Centre for Global Dialogue by Frost* Design uses quotation marks as an iconic symbol to represent dialogue and was used in the literature and print pieces produced for the organization. Here, it is used as a subtle tone on tone, but at a scale that fills the page.

Non-alphabetical typefaces (or Pi fonts)

These are made entirely of graphic characters and may include scientific symbols, arrows or symbols. The main use for these symbols is to add additional ideograms into legends or running text.

The massification of cell phones, texting and messaging has seen a new array of Pi fonts emerge called emoticons, face symbols that indicate emotion or feeling. These enable the writer of a brief message to readily communicate the emotional context of the message in shorthand. The reader thus has an idea of how serious or lighthearted a message is.

☎ to describe a service   ☞ to point the way   ❾ as a number in a list

✈ as a picture   ✳ as a symbol   ☺ to communicate emotion

Zapf Dingbats
An ever popular set of symbols.

Woodtype Ornaments
A set of symbols inspired by woodtype blocks including several 'printers hands'.

Restart
A series of hand drawn, sketch-like symbols.

Client: Self-published
Design: Gavin Ambrose and Matt Lumby
Typographic summary: Letters replaced with binary code

Typography | Non-alphabetical typefaces

American Psycho Binary

This is a version of *American Psycho* by Brett Eastern Ellis created by Gavin Ambrose and Matt Lumby that has been produced in binary. Each letter has been replaced by an 8-digit binary code that represents the letter. A side-effect of this is that the book contains eight times as many characters and runs to over 1,200 pages. Single words also have extended lengths so that in many cases only one word will fit to a line.

Industry view: Triboro

Tight budgets and copy-heavy content can leave little room for graphic intervention. But it is often when designers face the most severe constraints that the greatest creativity comes through in their work. Triboro often uses typography alone and its approach results in arresting pieces.

Typography features heavily in much of your work. What appeals to you about typographic forms?
We just love type; it's communication in its most basic form. When we start a project we begin with a blank page. The first action is to type or write the words we plan to use in the design. We usually recognize something interesting in that first step – and before we go down the path of organizing photoshoots or creating complex illustrations – we're already on the path of making something with type only.

What are the key considerations when using type as a visual element?
We often get wrapped up in trying to discover formal relationships hidden in words and letters. One game we play is to find links between letterforms and exaggerate these links. This is evident in early projects like our Air poster or David's signature (shown opposite top). Usually we start by looking at the letters present in the project and see if an opportunity emerges to create

some visual harmony. That was how we came to the Nike NYC logo (opposite bottom). Once we made the connection that both NIKE and NYC start with the letter 'N', we just asked if there was a way to unearth the 'Y' and the 'C' somehow, and fortunately the letters 'K' and 'E' made this possible. There is something fulfilling about exploiting to full effect these random 'discoveries'.

When designing with large amounts of text only information how do you add interest?
There's no one solution: breaking up layouts with white space, margins to frame typography, varying color and weight of typography to add emphasis. We try to put ourselves in the shoes of the reader and ask what can we do to entice someone to read it. Our mentor, Alexander Gelman, instilled in us the idea that typography is really about the structuring of information. It's architecture where words serve as your metal beams and concrete. The framework and structure you

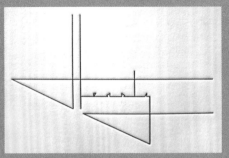

Above is a logo made from the signature of designer Heasty.

A poster (left) that is a typographic interpretation of pop group Air that featured in the music magazine Bigshot, that was inspired by contrails that airplanes leave in the atmosphere.

Pictured below is the logo for New York City meets Nike, that plays on Nike's well-known 'just do it' slogan by presenting a logo with a more 'do it yourself' style.

Industry view | Triboro

Paper of Record Pictured are images from an experimental series reimaging *New York Times* content via reader comments to create a shadow publication with an emphasis on democratic expression as readers determine the importance of stories based on the popularity of reader comments.

develop – we often use a lot of grids – will define the environment in which you encounter the language. For us hierarchy is key. As readers, we first scan the page quickly to orient ourselves, then we zoom in and start reading and appreciating the details within the layout. There is a micro and macro aspect to it that we would compare to wayfinding. In order to orient people you want to help them along as if you are designing signage in an airport. First, it should be clear to people where the bathrooms are, but when they get closer, they need to distinguish between the Women's and Men's room. Editorial design works similarly. You want to make it so people can easily distinguish between information that is relevant and interesting to them, and information that they can skip over.

How important is the personality that each typeface has? Are some personalities better and more useful than others?
We used to believe that a typeface's personality was secondary to the

structural and formal qualities of the layout, but we have become increasingly obsessed with trying to tailor typography to evoke very specific moods. Not surprisingly, this quest often leads us to have to create entirely new typefaces, as traits we are searching for may not be commercially available.

Regarding your question about typefaces that are more useful than others... I guess the easy answer is that faces that are neutral in personality and can be applied to a multitude of different projects. The elephant in the room with this is that the personality that I see in the type may not be seen by someone else. Nothing is universal. We heard a designer say recently that beauty should be avoided because beauty is subjective. This is bullshit. The pursuit of beauty, even on our own individual terms, is a worthy cause. When we arrive at something that we think is beautiful others will likely agree. Those that don't, don't. So what? Just because total consensus cannot be reached doesn't mean we should stop creating. We must create or die as somebody else put it.

Your use of typography stretches the gamut from clean to elaborate or complex. Do you instinctively know which approach to take or do you trial several different approaches?
I think we end up attacking most projects using both methods you describe. We may have a preconceived idea of an approach that might work best, but inevitably our projects usually end up being a winding journey where we second-guess ourselves and end up experimenting and testing multiple approaches. It's something we have to do as designers to get to a result we are happy with. Much in the same way that we are obsessing over the personality of faces, we are seeking the right aesthetic that we think best evokes the mood we want. If complexity benefits the design then we will try to push complexity to extremes but we're happy to pare things down to the most basic ingredients if this is what seems to make sense for the project.

Industry view | Triboro

Triboro is a Brooklyn based design duo of David Heasty and Stefanie Weigler that focuses on building inspiring brands from the ground-up and in shepherding established brands into new territories.

Client: JK& Magazine
Design: Triboro
Typographic summary:
Large scale type as a
picture object

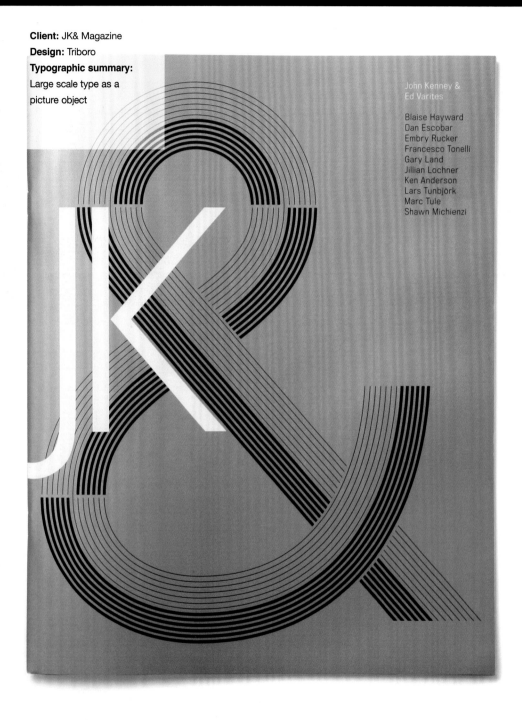

John Kenney &
Ed Varites

Blaise Hayward
Dan Escobar
Embry Rucker
Francesco Tonelli
Gary Land
Jillian Lochner
Ken Anderson
Lars Tunbjörk
Marc Tule
Shawn Michienzi

Setting type sounds straightforward enough – you put it down on the page and manipulate it – but the skill lies in knowing how to manipulate it to produce the results you require. To this end, there are various techniques and structures to help a designer control and set type effectively on the page. An understanding of these basics allows the designer to produce a coherent and effective design by controlling and harmonizing the various typographical elements that it contains.

The effective use of type is a combination of understanding typefaces –covered in the previous chapter – and controlling their usage to express the ideas that you want them to. Typography that is thoughtfully and precisely set will enhance the meaning of a given text. Even the relatively simple task of selecting a typeface requires informed decision making. Graphic communication is very much a sum of its parts and typeface selection can have a dramatic impact on a design, as the finer nuances of typesetting can alter the way we perceive and interpret messages. Thoughtful type setting facilitates the controlled imparting of information.

I do not think of type as something that should be readable. It should be beautiful.

Ed Benguiat

JK& Magazine

Pictured is the cover of a company magazine created for a photography agency by Triboro that features typography at a very large scale so that it stops being type and becomes a picture object.

Leading

Leading is a hot metal printing term that refers to the strips of lead that were inserted between text measures in order to space them accurately. Leading is specified in points and refers nowadays to the space between the lines of a text block. Leading introduces space into the text block and allows the characters to 'breathe' so that the information is easy to read.

To achieve a balanced and well-spaced text block, leading usually has a larger point size than the text it is associated with, for example a 12-point typeface might be set with 14-point leading.

8pt type on 8pt leading (set solid)

These text blocks demonstrate how the size of the leading affects the ability to read the text, and how it also affects the overall visual appearance.

Text set 8pt on 8pt is a very tight configuration.

8pt type on 9pt leading (set +1)

Text set 8pt on 9pt introduces more space between the text lines although it is still congested.

8pt type on 10pt leading (set +2)

Text set 8pt on 10pt is the optimal configuration in these examples as it provides sufficient space between lines for the text to be easy to read.

8pt type on 12pt leading (set +4)

The use of 12pt leading is too much for an 8pt typeface as it spaces the lines so that the connection between them starts to become lost and the eye has to leap from one to the next.

8pt type on 14pt leading (set +6)

Here – and in the example, shown right – leading opens up the text a bit too much as it looks over spaced.

8pt type on 16pt leading (set +8)

This additional space is distracting when reading a paragraph of type as the gap is uncomfortably large when moving from line to line.

Client: Fake London Genius
Design: Browns
Typographic summary:
Negative leading to create
tapestry effect

Showrooms
UK// Four Marketing
Phone +44 20 7287 6767
Contact Nicky Goodman
Italy// Future Net
Phone +39 02 89 400 143
Contact Tommaso Pezzato
Japan// Jack Of All Trades
Phone +81 3 3470 0990
Contact Hiroshi Teraoka
Greece// Exit
Phone +30 21 0813 1555
Contact Angelo Kuronomos
Spain// Vasmanche
Phone +34 91 527 90 56
Contact Regina Trevino
Germany// Agentur Toepfer
Phone +49 211 13 06 36 0
Contact Udo Toepfer

Portugal// Correa Telehnas
Phone +351 213 651 000
Contact Anabela Borges
Benelux// Moshi Moshi
Phone +31 20 68 85 818
Contact Alex Jaspers
Australia/New Zealand// R3 FM
Phone +61 283 99 39 45
Contact Ben Rennie
Switzerland/Austria// Madisons
Phone +41 17 229 191
Contact Patrick Ebonether
USA// Four Marketing
Phone +44 7801 480 109
Contact Ollie Amhurst

Fake London Genius

This Spring / Summer 2005 brochure for Fake
London Genius features text that is set with tight,
negative leading, which results in the ascenders
butting into the baseline of the line above. This
creates a fabric/tapestry effect due to the use of a
sans serif typeface that is alternately colored in
red and black.

Typography | Leading

Tracking

Tracking refers to the amount of space that exists between letters. This space can be adjusted to make characters more or less distinguishable. Reducing the tracking pares back the space between letters, condenses the text and may allow more text to be fitted into a given area.

However, if tracking is reduced too much the letters begin to 'crash' into one another. Also, space should not be added to the extent that letters become separated from the words that they are part of.

Typographic color refers to the density of a typeface, and the denser it is, the more space it fills or colors. Due to this, type can be used to color a space as well as impart information.

Normal tracking

This is Garamond Book with normal tracking.

Loose tracking

This is the same typeface set with loose tracking. This is sometimes referred to as letterspacing.

Tight tracking

This is the same typeface set with tight tracking.

Negative tracking

This removes the space between letters so that they touch and bunch up.

Tracking values will affect a whole text block and apply a 'blanket' value to all characters within it. This block is set with a value of -30pt, which creates a block of tightly set text. This is described as being 'darker', as there is a greater proportion of black (type) to white (space).

In contrast a 'lighter' setting is one in which the amount of white space to black type is increased. This text block is set with a value of +60pt, which creates 'looser' set text, with a lighter overall appearance.

-12pt

When reproduced in a smaller point size, the visual difference becomes more apparent. The more the tracking is reduced, the 'darker' the overall appearance, while a lighter feel is attained using an 'open' tracking value.

0pt

When reproduced in a smaller point size, the visual difference becomes more apparent. The more the tracking is reduced, the 'darker' the overall appearance, while a lighter feel is attained using an 'open' tracking value.

+12pt

When reproduced in a smaller point size, the visual difference becomes more apparent. The more the tracking is reduced, the 'darker' the overall appearance, while a lighter feel is attained using an 'open' tracking value.

Typography | Tracking

When setting text reversed out of black or a color block you need to add tracking to compensate for the 'creep' of ink.

Thin typefaces can appear 'broken' when reversed, and for this reason heavier weight versions of a font are used. The second paragraph here is set in a heavier version of Helvetica Neue.

Client: Royal Society of Arts
Design: NB: Studio
Typographic summary:
16-page brochure and
broadsheet poster featuring
small-point type

The way the RS
means that as
I get to talk to
in different fiel
would never

Dr Nicholas Baldwin,
Dean and Director of Operati
Wroxton College of Fairleigh
Dickinson University

vorks
ellow
ny people
, whom I
rmally meet...

Royal Society of Arts
To do something slightly different for this RSA 16-page brochure – containing a series of illustrations by Tom Gauld – NB: Studio created a broadsheet poster to wrap around and so contain the booklet. The poster carries all the names of the fellows of the society. There are literally thousands of these names to incorporate, which not only indicates the popularity and importance of the organization but also, on a more practical level, demanded the use of a very small point size in order to print all the information.

A simple hierarchy of 'pattern' and 'text' is created through the variety of typesizes. Although all the text can be read, it's not intended that all the text should be read, and the dramatic differences in size help to enforce this.

Kerning

Kerning refers to the space between two letters. Certain combinations have too much or little space between them making some words difficult to read, so you focus on the typographical 'mistakes'.

This problem can be reduced by kerning, the removal or addition of space between letters. Some letter combinations frequently need to be kerned and are known as kerning pairs. Kerning is used to achieve a balanced look for larger display type, and to handle difficult combinations of letters in body copy.

airport

airport

There are two important rules to remember when kerning text:

1
As type size increases you need to reduce spacing to compensate. The words above have the same relative kerning values. The top word looks correctly set but the bottom one looks 'loose' in the middle section and should be kerned in. The top word has additional spacing entered between the 'r' and 't'.

2
Do not kern until the tracking values and typeface selections have been set, as time-consuming fine-adjustments could easily be wasted by a later change. Do not assume that one set of values transfers to another typeface as different typefaces need bespoke kerning.

Even a single word can require a lot of kerning. When kerning, you need to identify the problem areas. In the example below, there is a collapse of space around the 'r' and 'n', but also a surprising amount of space between other letters that can be taken out to balance the letterforms.

Kerning
Kerning

-30pt   -21pt   +10pt   -40pt   -29pt

Serif fonts require careful consideration as the serifs can extenuate the effect of letters collapsing into one another. In the example below, certain letter pairs are becoming joined, while space opens between others. In extreme instances you may need to use a dotless 'i' or a ligature to achieve balance.

Kerning
Kerning

-30pt -5pt   -5pt   +40pt 0pt   -40pt

Client: Aram Store
Design: Studio Myerscough
Typographic summary:
Angular typeface, kerned
back

Aram Store
This logo for Aram Store by Studio Myerscough features letters that have been kerned back to the point that they just touch. This works because the typeface is angular and solid and so the contact surface is minimal.

Client: Cobella

Design: NB: Studio

Typographic summary: Avant Garde employed as a display type with negative kerning

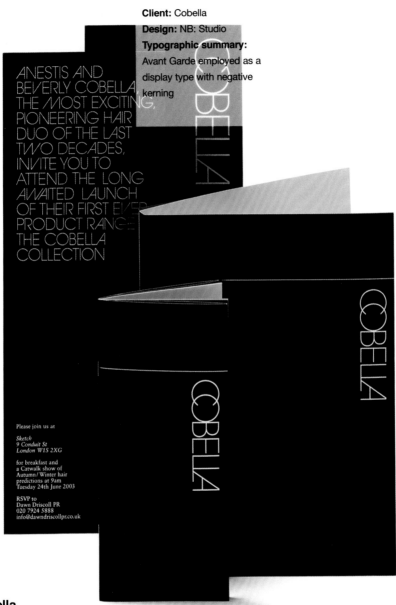

ANESTIS AND BEVERLY COBELLA THE MOST EXCITING, PIONEERING HAIR DUO OF THE LAST TWO DECADES, INVITE YOU TO ATTEND THE LONG AWAITED LAUNCH OF THEIR FIRST EVER PRODUCT RANGE THE COBELLA COLLECTION

Please join us at

Sketch
9 Conduit St
London W1S 2XG

for breakfast and
a Catwalk show of
Autumn/ Winter hair
predictions at 9am
Tuesday 24th June 2003

RSVP to
Dawn Driscoll PR
020 7924 5888
info@dawndriscollpr.co.uk

/ **Typography** | Kerning

Cobella

To create an identity for a range of hair products by Cobella, NB: Studio used an alternative, display type version of Avant Garde. The standard has upright versions of characters such as 'A', 'M', 'V' and 'W'. The distinctive forward sloping of these characters within the typeface create individuality but not necessarily legibility. The use of Avant Garde is restricted to a display function and Bell Gothic is used for typesetting additional information. The main logotype is set with negative kerning, which again increases distinction and personality.

Type spacing choices

This is Swiss monospaced type, each character occupies the same width and so it demands more space than other type.

Type spacing choices

This is Swiss proportionally-spaced type, as the letter spacing is proportional to the letter size the text string is more compact and uses less space.

Each of the characters in monospaced typefaces occupies the same width, irrespective of its actual size. These typefaces were originally used on typewriters as they enable the creation of text that aligns in vertical columns to be easily produced. Courier is an example of a monospaced typeface that has become popular in the digital age. The disadvantage of monospaced type is that it appears mechanical, is hard to read and occupies a great deal of space.

Proportionally-spaced type uses a spacing system that was developed by the Monotype and Linotype type foundries, which mimics the letterspacing of historical handset forms. Individual characters occupy a space proportional to their size, this makes text easier to read and means it takes up less space. However, it is more difficult to align numerals or text vertically if using a proportionally-spaced typeface.

The use of non-standard capitalization is increasingly popular in order to create distinguishing points in designs and trademarked terms; for example PostScript. This is referred to as intercaps, bicapitalization or camel case and is characterized by the joining of compound words or phrases without spacing, crucially, each term is capitalized. The uneven profile of such words has a supposed resemblance to the humps of a Bactrian camel.

CamelCase

Client: Everything in
Between
Design: 3 Deep
Typographic summary:
Colliding words, highlighted
type

hellogoodbye
beginningend
monologuedialogue

everythingbetween

Brett Phillips
Program Director
everything@3deep.com.au

hellogoodbye
beginningend
monologuedialogue
reactionaction
fictiontruth

everythingbetween

hellogoodbye
beginningend
monologuedialogue
reactionaction
fictiontruth

everythingbetween

With compliments

Everything in Between

This stationery identity for Everything in Between by 3 Deep features the collision of words running into one another without spacing which provides sound-bite messages such as 'hellogoodbye', 'beginningend', 'fictiontruth' and so on. This approach is also incorporated into the company's logo; 'everythingbetween' as 'in' is highlighted in a different color.

Typography | Spacing

Overprinting and knocking out

Traditional four-color printing can be restrictive. Black, printed on its own, can appear flat and insubstantial. Overprinting can overcome this problem and add creative layering. To understand overprinting, however, one needs a basic understanding of a process called 'knocking out'.

(Above) As the cyan plate overlaps the magenta and yellow plates the type is 'knocked out' leaving the three colors intact (i.e. solid and not combined or mixed). Shown to the right is a block of solid black ink printed separately, notice the lighter density of the ink color.

An overprint (or surprint), describes a process where one color prints directly over the previous colors in the cyan, magenta, yellow and black print order (above). Where one color overlaps another, both colors print, resulting in a combination of the colors. The black square to the right is printed using all four colors; this is called a four-color black as it has more density than a single print black box above it. This technique of overprinting can be used to add texture to a design.

Metropolis (right)
This newsletter for Metropolis Bookstore by 3 Deep uses a series of overprints. The body text overprints green section headers adding a textural highlight to the columns. By overprinting the darker color over the lighter, you eliminate mis-registration problems; where slithers of white show if the plates don't marry up.

Client: Metropolis Bookstore
Design: 3 Deep
Typographic summary:
Large-point headers
overprinted in color

Fruits
Shoichi Aoki
Phaidon
Coming soon
$55.00 approximately

Fabric of Fashion
British Council
Coming soon
$50.00 approximately

Thomas Demand
Francesco Bonami, Regis Durand
Thames and Hudson
Available now
$60.00 approximately

The Best from Twenty Years of i-D
Terry Jones
Taschen
Coming soon
$100.00 approximately

Facsimile
Francis Bernhoud
Edition Dino Simonet
Coming soon
$70.00 approximately

Photographs
Abbas Kiarostami
Hazan
Coming soon
$60.00 approximately

Objects to Use
Ole Bakker
010
Coming Soon
$75.00 approximately

Industrial Design
Jasper Morrison
Lars Muller
Coming soon
$200.00 approximately

Matzpark: A House Like Me
Michael McDonough
Clarkson N. Potter
Available now
$120.00 approximately

The Activist Drawing: Retracing Situationist Architectures from Constant's New Babylon to Beyond
Catherine de Zegher, Mark Wigley
MIT Press
Coming soon
$70.00 approximately

Inside Cars
J. Abbott Miller
Princeton Architectural Press
Coming soon
$40.00 approximately

Integral Ruedi Baur at Associes
Lars Muller
Coming Soon
$120.00 approximately

3D-2D/Designers Republic
Ole Bouman, Jeffery Kipnis
Laurence King
$120.00 approximately

Colours: Rem Koolhaas/OMA, Norman Foster, Alessandro Mendini
Birkhauser
Coming soon
$30.00 approximately

Zines
Coming Soon
$90.00 approximately

Architecture Goes Wild - Manifest Writings
Kas Oosterhuis
010
Coming soon
$100.00 approximately

Extreme Canvas: Movie Poster Paintings from Ghana
Ernie Wolfe III
Dilettante Press
Available now
$100.00 approximately

It Crossed My Mind
Marijke Van Warmerdom
Octagon
Available now
$75.00 approximately

Metropolis Studio Application Form
Name
Address
Telephone
Email
Profession

Paintings, Photographs, Films
Dennis Hopper
Stedelik Museum
Coming soon
$60.00 approximately

Hitchcock and Art - Fatal Coincidences
Mazzotta Editore
Coming Soon
$100.00 approximately

Senses of Cinema

Legibility and readability

These two terms are often used synonymously, however, legibility refers to the ability to distinguish one letterform from another through the physical characteristics inherent in the design of a particular typeface, such as x-height, counter size, stroke contrast, and type weight. The legibility of a text also depends upon aspects such as leading and alignment. Absolute clarity of information combined with a minimum of interfering factors creates legible type.

Readability concerns the properties of a piece of type or design that affect the ability to 'understand' it and shapes our opinions about the information it contains.

Cognitive meaning
The cognitive meaning of an object or image is what we have learnt to know or understand from looking at it. For example we have learned that red is associated with danger and that '?' means a question has been asked.

Denotative meaning
Images are often used because they explicitly denote or designate something. For example, an image of a musical instrument denotes that the subject relates to music.

Client: Who's Next
Design: Research Studios
Typographic summary:
Sans serif text as a graphic
device that intentionally
reduces readability

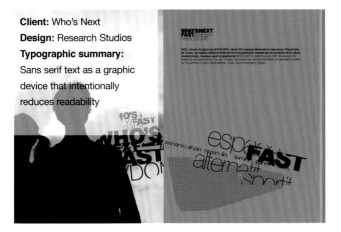

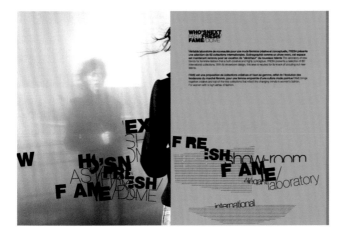

Who's Next

This corporate identity
was designed by
Research Studios for
Who's Next; a top
international fashion
event held in France.
The commercial guide
pictured features
disjointed typography,
which is used as a
graphical device so that
the letters of a word do
not track in an expected
manner, resulting in
diminished readability.
The use of different sizes
and weights further
compounds this.
However, as the text
is used as a graphical
device, readability of
the complete text string
is secondary in
importance to the
individual words. These
jump out at the reader,
as a result of this styling,
and shout 'Fast', 'Fresh',
'Fame' and 'Dome'.

Typography | Legibility and readability

Client: This is a Magazine
Design: Studio KA
Typographic summary:
Text lines form a woman,
point size creates 'lines'
with different thickness

This is a Magazine

This design by Studio KA uses typography to create an image of a woman dancing. The lines of text are bent, curved and truncated to form the lines of the figure. Type point size also varies to create 'lines' with different thicknesses.

Client: Levi's
Design: The Kitchen
Typographic summary:
Hand-drawn to provide
anarchic characteristics

Levi's

This brochure for clothing manufacturer Levi's by The Kitchen, uses 'Sonic Revolution' as the central theme of the clothing styles it displays. The design features aggressive and anarchic hand-drawn type to convey these qualities and associate them with the clothing brand. The design also mimics the diary or journal of a teenager, enforcing the target market for the clothing.

The cover is produced on a thin bible-paper stock that contrasts with the glossy inner pages.

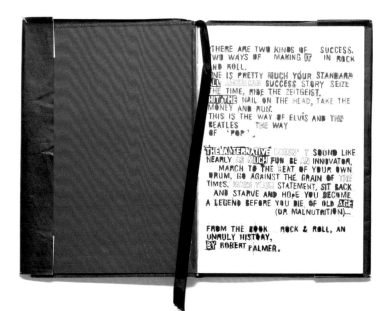

Typography | Legibility and readability

Industry view: Designbolaget

A good designer can seemingly work miracles with very little, creating a striking design with a minimum of strokes. Such situations call for the utmost innovation and non-linear thought processes, such as the examples shown here from Designbolaget, which produced a whole series of covers using a black rectangle shape. What at first appears simplistic actually draws extensively upon art history and in particular Modernists such as Piet Mondrian and Armin Hoffman. While not every viewer will pick up such references, there is a thought process at work that ensures a level of consistency and coherence from cover to cover.

There is a skill in setting type so that it both communicates and looks interesting. What is your approach to this formidable challenge?

When working with type we try out a lot of ways of organizing the type to work with its message and any image material it might be connected with. We try to look at the material and see if there is a little 'gift' in the way the words can connect with each other or maybe we can play around with the hierarchy of the words. Often the solution is in the material itself. Other than that we make sure it 'sits' properly and is kerned the way we want.

In your work for Funen Art Academy, a line serves as a counterpoint to enliven what would otherwise be quite sparse covers. What influences the development of this kind of graphic intervention?

We prefer to work with simple graphics that have a function and strengthen the message instead of loading on a lot of elements just for decoration. When it came to the identity for Funen Art Academy's degree show it was important that it could represent all of the graduates exhibited, and in this we needed to 'step back' from the material. The lines represent a count-down but also the number of students graduating.

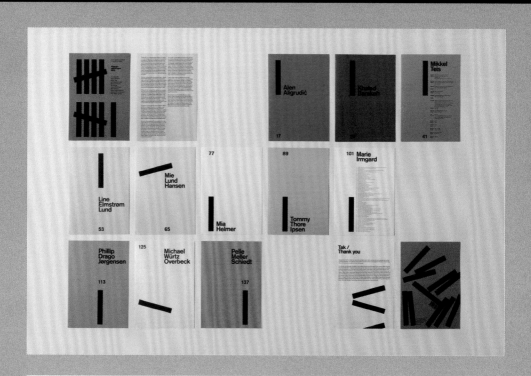

Industry view | Designbolaget

Covers for the Funen Art Academy degree show feature a line motiff used in multiple ways to differentiate each student.

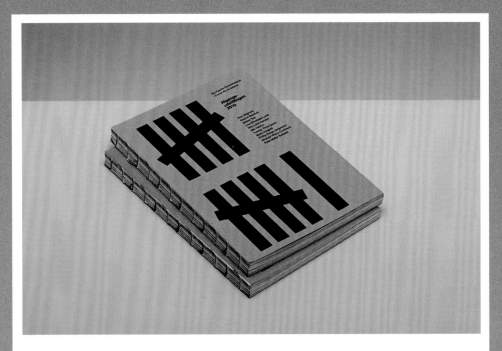

Which Modernist designers influence your approach to work?
Of course we have some designers that we love the work of, especially the old iconic designers, but we are inspired by movements rather than specific designers.

What advice would you give young designers who face the challenge of having to design something with a very limited range of tools such as the Funen Art Academy covers?

Having a limited range of tools doesn't necessarily mean you can't make good design. We believe that few elements and a concept/ idea that works well will get you a long way. You don't need to choose the most expensive materials to achieve great results, but rather look at accessible materials and highlight their qualities by good design that works.

Designbolaget is a Copenhagen-based graphic design studio founded in 2002 by Claus Due that works at the intersections of art, fashion and culture. The studio believes in conceptual thinking and original ideas to design bespoke solutions, with a focus on printed matter.

Covers for the Funen Art Academy degree show and the booklets bound together with an uncovered spine.

Industry view | Designbolaget

Fiction
New Work by BalletLab

Venue
Chunky Move
111 Sturt Street
Southbank VIC
Reservations
CUB Malthouse
9685 5111
Tickets
$20 Full
$15 Concession

Dates
Thursday 19th – Saturday
21st August at 8.30pm
Tuesday 24th – Saturday
28th August at 8.30pm
Sunday 29th August at 5pm
Post show forum Tuesday
24th August

Choreography
Phillip Adams and
Rebecca Hilton
Live sound composition
Lynton Carr
Performers
Brooke Stamp, Ryan Lowe
Carlee Mellow, Joanne
White, Tim Harvey,
Clair Peters and Edgar
John Wegner

Lighting
Ben Cisterne
Costumes
Graham Green
Graphic Design
3 Deep Design
Photography
Jeff Busby

Client: Balletlab
Design: 3 Deep
Typographic summary:
Typeface generated from
background pattern

Type generation refers to the different approaches used to create letterforms whether as part of a deliberate and involved process to design a new typeface or simply spray-painting letters. The unifying theme in this chapter is that typography may be constructed and manipulated in many ways and taken from different sources to serve specific design purposes. As such, designers harness the attributes in the generated type to add to, or reinforce, the message they want to convey.

Bespoke type generation can result in something unique and personal, and might meet the needs of a client seeking to create a new identity.

The examples in this chapter demonstrate some of the many ways of approaching type generation including hand-drawn type, building letterforms and font generation. Whether using exacting and complex grid formations or more basic mark-making techniques, type generation can offer benefits over existing commercial typefaces. Although many of these examples are experimental, the basic principles remain valid as they are produced within the larger context of typographical conventions, even if they push the boundaries.

The first time I drew type I felt like I was standing at the bottom of Mount Everest wearing a swimsuit. Nina Stössinger

Balletlab
Created for Balletlab by 3 Deep, this poster uses a typeface that was developed from the background pattern. The pattern limits the character shapes that can be produced and provides an inclined baseline for the text. The result is text that is dynamic, contemporary and evocative of the subject matter it conveys.

Hand-drawn type

Typography starts with characters that are shapes that can be drawn or crafted, but whereas this process to create new typefaces was once a manual, hand-drawn process, technology has taken over and today digital typefaces mimic the human hand as shown below.

Although there have been many attempts to emulate handwriting in type, nothing can reproduce those inherent idiosyncrasies generated from changes in pressure, speed and concentration that grace handwritten script.

abcdefghijklmnopqrstuvwxyz

Pepita
Designed in 1959 by Imre Reiner for the Monotype, Pepita simulates the spontaneous strokes of the written word.

abcdefghijklmnopqrstuvwxyz

Biffo
David Marshall created Biffo in 1964. This typeface emulates the strokes of a broad-tipped pen as can be seen in the round and flexible figures. Vertical strokes have rounded edges that soften the characters. Biffo is suitable for short and mid-length texts as well as headlines.

abcdefghijklmnopqrstuvwxyz

Snell Roundhand
Snell Roundhand was designed in 1965 by Matthew Carter and is based on 18th century round-hand scripts. It has an elegant and festive feel that is suited to mid-length texts and headlines.

Client: Coexistence
Design: Studio Myerscough
Typographic summary:
Hand-drawn type, ragged
lines, different point sizes

Typography | Hand-drawn type

Coexistence
To create the identity for furniture company Coexistence, Studio Myerscough
used hand-drawn letters with intentionally rough edges, that were set in different
point sizes and overlapped one another. The almost brutal handling of the
typography makes a strong counterpoint to the refined lines of the furniture. The
immediacy of the typography also conveys a playful sense of 'sketch', reminding
us of the designed and bespoke nature of the product.

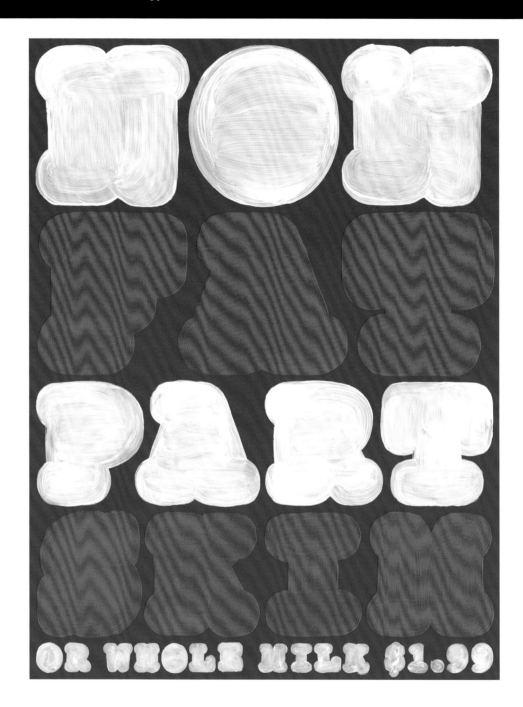

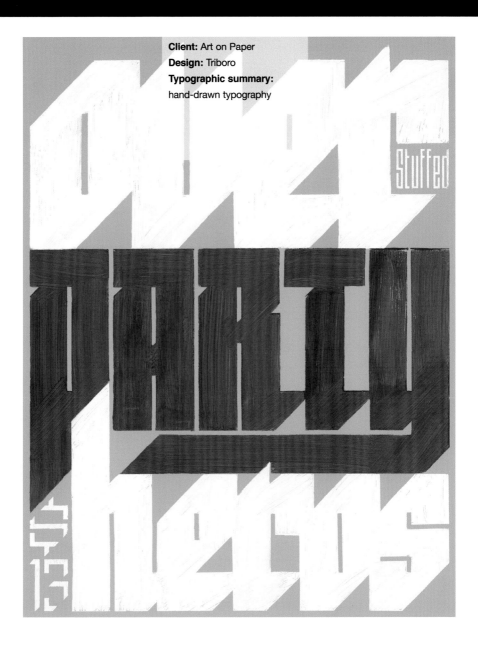

Client: Art on Paper
Design: Triboro
Typographic summary:
hand-drawn typography

Typography | Hand-drawn type

Supermarket Series

Pictured are hand-painted posters created by Triboro for the Art on Paper Great Poster project that reimagine supermarket advertisements and feature hand-drawn bespoke typography. The characters do not have the same legibility that we are used to in product packaging and cause the viewer to work harder to receive the message, the opposite of what packaging actually does.

Building letterforms

Designers can take a more structured approach to building letterforms by using a grid or other structure to help define and determine their strokes. While still created by hand, this approach allows for consistent characteristics to be imposed on the letterforms and means that a designer does not have to contemplate each and every stroke of each and every letter, thus speeding up the process. The development of geometric typefaces such as those that came out of the Bauhaus in the early twentieth century provides an example of characters that were built up.

Jeff Busby (opposite)

This identity for photographer Jeff Busby, by 3 Deep uses a strong geometric grid from which the letterforms are built. This restricts the shape of the characters but results in something unique for the client.

Client: Jeff Busby
Design: 3 Deep
Typographic summary:
Font drawn on to geometric
grid, shapes restricted

Client: Metropolitan Workshop
Design: Gavin Ambrose /
Urbik / Daniel Glazebrook
Typographic summary:
Typographic identity
developed from an
architectural approach

Metropolitan Workshop

Metropolitan Workshop

The development of unique letterforms can be useful in creating a sense of identity. This example was developed by Gavin Ambrose, Urbik and Daniel Glazebrook for an architecture practice, whereby the letterforms mirror or hint at the shapes found in different approaches to architecture. The logo and typographic development was undertaken through a series of workshops with staff from the architects' practice, and thus also served as a mechanism for inclusion and ownership by all.

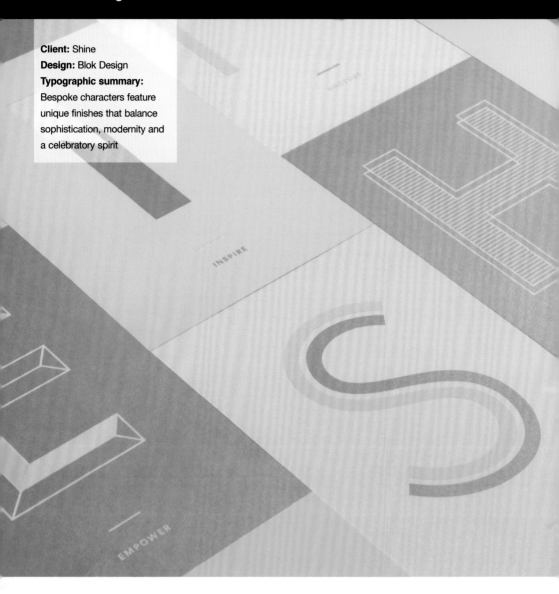

Client: Shine
Design: Blok Design
Typographic summary:
Bespoke characters feature
unique finishes that balance
sophistication, modernity and
a celebratory spirit

Shine

Pictured is specially designed typography created by Blok Design to celebrate and honor the first graduating class of Manifestworks, a job training workshop for the film industry that helps youth emerging from foster care and the criminal justice system. The bespoke characters were constructed to feature unique strokes, finishes and bold color that balance sophistication and modernity with a celebratory spirit.

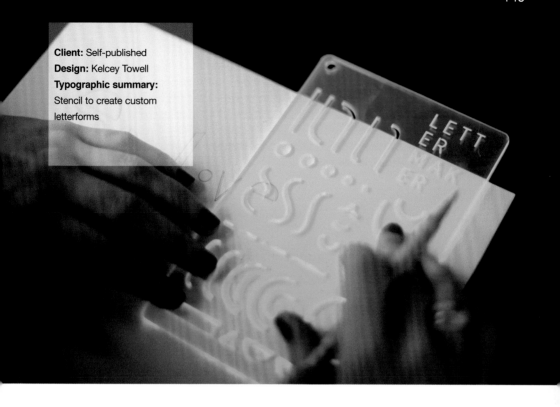

Client: Self-published
Design: Kelcey Towell
Typographic summary:
Stencil to create custom
letterforms

Typography | Building letterforms

LetterMaker

Pictured is a lettering tool called the *LetterMaker* created by Kelcey Towell that is
a stencil that isolates the basic forms of typography and allows anyone to create
custom letterforms. It was developed so that people of all ages, designers and
non-designers, could explore the possibility of typography, utilize legibility (or
not!) and communication, and to play with form, collage and mark-making.

Sweden

Pictured is Swedish Sans, a bespoke typeface created by Söderhavet and Stefan Hattenbach for the government of Sweden that has geometric features and a soft tonality to enable it to be used across various different state agencies. "We work with design drivers based on the company values to set the tonality of a typeface. It's not the easiest part of a design brief to fulfill but we are close to having set a process model in place that works for us," expains Jesper Robinell of Söderhavet and Stefan Hattenbach.

Sweden
Sans©

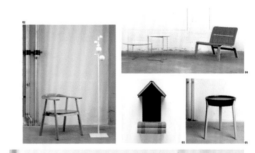

Swedish Design Goes Milan   - Participants / David design

DAVID
DESIGN

—

It has now been over 25 years since a new era of Scandinavian design began.

David design was among the first Swedish brands to internationally promote this new simple, minimalistic and sustainable Scandinavian design style.

David design, the renowned manufacturer of contemporary furniture design, celebrates 2013 with the Collage Collection. Collage meaning that you will see most complete collection ever from this groundbreaking company.

New design from Nendo, Claesson Koivisto Rune, Andreas Engesvik, Luca Nichetto, Patty Johnson and Federico Churba show together with previous products from Inga Sempé, Richard Hutten, Benjamin Hubert, Mats Theselius and more, to give a complete collage for home and contract market.

Today David design is an international brand, catering for customers looking for iconic, functional and sustainable furniture and design accessories. Some of the world's leading designers are collaborating with David design, which is represented by some of the top international retailers.

- Photos
01. Collage sofa system and Oblique mirror
02. Chair Haida and clothhanger Oak
03. Random seat
04. Tray table Bailey, Readers nest and easy chair Boxen
05. Sidetable Cocrete

Client: Government of
Sweden
Design: Söderhavet and
Stefan Hattenbach
Typographic summary:
Bespoke characters

Font generation

Although there are thousands of different typefaces it is sometimes still necessary to create a new one. The ultimate aim of font generation is often to produce a fully functioning typeface. A full set of upper and lower case characters with punctuation, numerals and all the associated glyphs can run into hundreds of characters although many working typefaces are reduced to a simpler set, for example uppercase only.

The motivation for undertaking this effort is usually to create a unique, bespoke, typographical solution. The examples shown within these spreads have been constructed, built, rendered and created for specific applications. Many of these examples not only result in engaging designs, but also challenge the fabric of what we may feel constitutes a typeface.

Made in Clerkenwell (right)

This typeface by Research Studios was designed to promote 'Made in Clerkenwell', an open event in central London. To reflect the precise and crafted artisanal nature of the works to be exhibited (that included ceramics, textiles and jewelry), a hand-drawn type was developed.

The typeface was generated using vector paths that can be quickly manipulated to obtain the desired shape and style for each letter using lines of the same width to ensure consistency and a degree of uniformity from letter to letter.

Client: Clerkenwell Studios
Design: Research Studios
Typographic summary:
Hand-drawn type, vector
paths

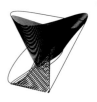

Typography | Font generation

Client: Matt Alberts
Design: Planning Unit
Typographic summary:
Bespoke sans serif types
for subculture photography
book

Client: NOAM
Design: Graphical House
Typographic summary:
Custom stencil typeface

Typography | Font generation

NOAM (above)

Pictured is a brand redesign for high-quality luxury interiors design studio NOAM, created by Graphical House, that features an understated identity and a custom stencil typeface. The brand design and custom typeface aim to articulate the precise and deliberate attention to detail and finesse present in spaces created by NOAM. This example also highlights that the complexities of developing a working typeface are compounded when you also have to factor in the development of additional weights.

Soapbox and Dogfight (opposite)

Pictured (top) is Soapbox, one of two bespoke title fonts created by Planning Unit for The Seasons Collection book by photographer Matt Alberts about skate and surf culture. The second font is Dogfight (pictured bottom). Dogfight and Soapbox are used for the headlines and section dividers to add a voice and character to the compilation of images.

Dynamic type for the screen

Many designers increasingly design for digital or screen applications rather than for print production. While many type setting conventions are equally valid in the digital/screen space, a designer needs to understand other considerations, particularly that screen applications often feature movement. Typefaces are now developed specifically to work with the demands and possibilities of being viewed on screens and as such, type design continues to evolve to meet new challenges.

Digital and analog

While types are designed specifically for the digital space, dynamic type does not necessarily have to be digital in construction and analog, or process work can still be used. This combination of styles and approaches can result in the creation of more dynamic work.

Black Farmer (right)

Pictured are stills from an animated advertisement created by Planning Unit and Tony Kaye for Wilfred Emmanuel-Jones, AKA The Black Farmer, that features various typographic treatments created with analog type used to help make things that appear to be uncool cool and different from the standard food ad.

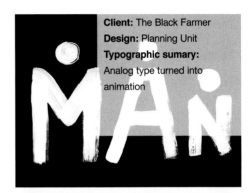

Client: The Black Farmer
Design: Planning Unit
Typographic sumary:
Analog type turned into animation

Typography | Dynamic type for the screen

Client: DK&A
Design: NB: Studio
Typographic sumary:
Ampersand as keystone
in visual identity

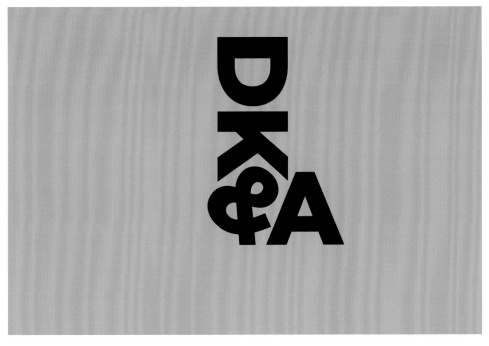

Typography | Dynamic type for the screen

DK&A

Pictured are images from a brand design created by NB: Studio for London-based strategy studio DK&A founded by former chief executive of the Design Council David Kester. The company refers to itself as a 'curious hybrid', which formed the basis of the resolution of the brief, that makes a hero of the ampersand and charges it with a unique magnetism as a visual metaphor for what Kester does best: using his personality to bring together people and ideas around a problem that needs a solution. This can be seen in the quirky orientation of the ampersand in the company name, rotated upon its chin.

Industry view: Leftloft

Leftloft is not afraid of a challenge, such as updating a typographical classic: Helvetica. Here we look at the process and decisions behind such a bold move.

Why update Helvetica? What were the key challenges?

Etica was the type debut of a young studio. As young designers, we were full of new inputs and we were looking for our own personality. In this sense, Etica was a sort of studio manifesto: we were fascinated by the design classics of the sixties, of the International Style, of Modernism, which was the cultural backbone we've been trained with. Helvetica represents the typographic embodiment of Modernism: beautiful but old; cool but incapable of describing present times. We decided to interpret this change through typography and design something that had the same ability of 'filling the space' that Helvetica has without being the same thing. We named it Etica, as though Etica was the feminine part of Helvetica that set herself free from the tyrannical Modernist Helv!

What adaptations did you make to ensure Etica's utility in the digital space? What are the challenges of designing type for digital?

When we designed Etica, we were not thinking about its use on digital devices. To be sincere, displays nowadays perform so well that when designing for that particular purpose you only need to bear in mind some basic typographic ingredients to guarantee better performance in extreme viewing conditions (poor light, small type). A few years ago this was not the case and most typefaces without proper 'hinting' instructions were barely readable. Now technology helps us a lot. For Etica in particular, Typekit prepared a more precisely hinted version since the service they provided was essentially web-oriented.

Leftloft is an independent studio founded in Milan, Italy in 2009 and with an office in Brooklyn, NY that works internationally, to fuse European and North American perspectives into the creation of visual identities, design experiences and digital solutions while pushing the edge of creative research.

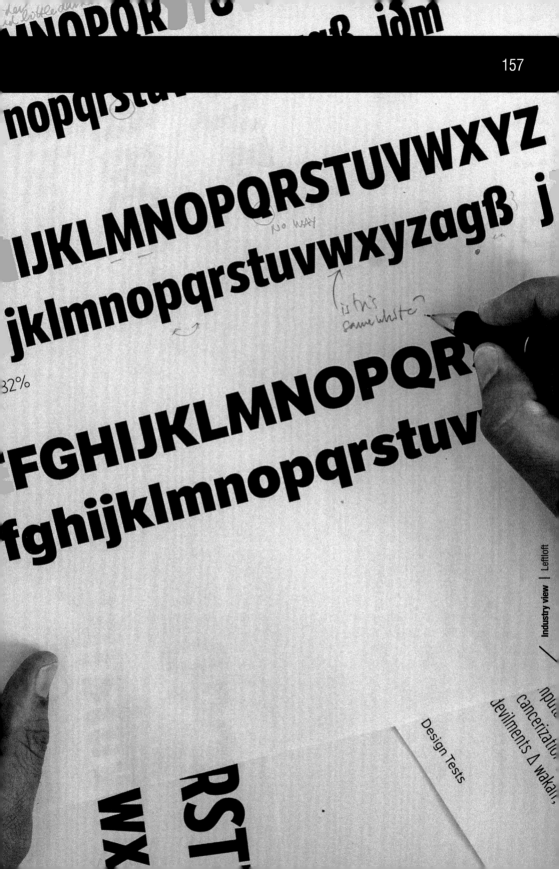

Björkma

Björkma

Font hinting or instructing uses mathematical instructions to adjust the display of an outline font so that it lines up with a rasterized grid, to help make characters clear and legible.

Typefaces are as susceptible to fashion as other aspects of design. To what extent is it necessary to revisit established, classic typefaces so that they remain current and relevant?
Revisitation of type classics is as necessary as conceiving completely new ones. The redesign is just one way of having ideas. It might be vital for conveying an idea or be a starting point (as in the case of Etica) and during the process, it becomes something else and brand new.

Is there a need for letterforms to adapt to changes in how people communicate?
Absolutely! Even if typography is one of the most conservative visual disciplines, it changes continuously. What I always say to people asking why we need new typefaces is that we need them for the same reason that we need new music, novels or works of art; we need new alphabets to be able to describe present times. The other is because a complex system of communication, like a newspaper or an environment, needs complete and custom tools. There may be no typefaces able to solve a specific design issue – a

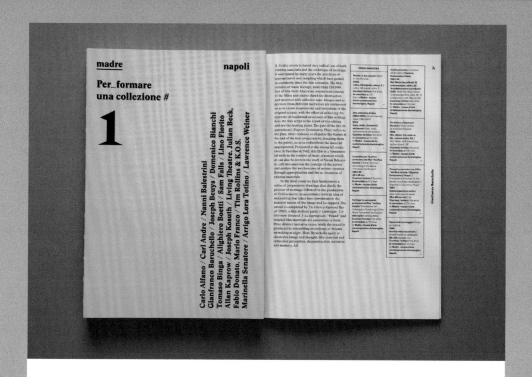

style is missing or a specific feature is not there – and sometimes it's faster and better performing to design something tailor made. The advent of the digital world changed the way typefaces are designed, produced and sold. In a word, everything has changed and digital processes have also impacted on letterforms. If you just think about generative design and coding applied to type, you can understand how big the change is.

In more type-related terms, the end of Modernism leads typography to bend towards an old but new architecture of letters such as the new breed of humanist typefaces, as opposed to rationalist ones, that led the way during the second part of the last century. Open contours, calligraphic heritage as opposed to 'mechanized' typography of the modernist type.

Which serif typeface would you like to rework?

It depends on the goal of the design. But, I'd like to work on one of the italics that Francesco Griffo designed for Aldus Manutius. I've been always intrigued by Griffo as a person. He was born in my hometown (Bologna) and he was likely sentenced to death for the killing of his son-in-law, but most of all because he designed amazing letters that influenced typographers for centuries.

Industry view | Leftloft

Client: The Photographers' Gallery
Design: Spin
Typographic summary: Large sans serif, overprinting images

Chapter 6

Type realization

With a solid grasp of typographical basics a designer can start to use the other key elements of the design process to enhance them. This chapter addresses type realization and how the production of a job can add additional qualities to typographical elements, such as tactile qualities achieved through substrate selection or printing choices.

The subtle differences offered by printing techniques and substrate selection can be powerful differentiators. In the following examples, the typesetting is generally restrained, yet the work is surprisingly distinctive and imaginative. The 'realization' of the work is equally important to the typesetting and the two shouldn't be thought of as being separable.

Although most printed work is four-color print on an uninspiring stock, there are many opportunities to break from this norm. From simple appropriations of printing techniques, like the overprinting in the example opposite, or more radical departures into unusual stocks, type realization is the point that a piece can truly come alive.

The beauty of type lies in its utility; *prettiness* without readability serves neither author *nor* reader. James Felici

The Photographers' Gallery

This information mailer for The Photographers' Gallery uses a Gothic typeface that overprints (see page 124) the images underneath it. The images underlying the text could affect the ease of reading it, but its large point size means this is not problematic and creates a textural quality to the piece.

Materials

How a design will appear depends to a large extent on the substrate on which it is placed. There is a vast array of materials available to a designer, many of which will have practical aspects to take into consideration in addition to their visual qualities.

Different paper substrates absorb different amounts of ink and vary in gloss and reflectiveness, for example. Of course, paper may not be the substrate chosen, as most surfaces will take a printed image though not all can pass through a printer. The examples that follow show how non-paper substrates can be used to great effect.

A Flock of Words (right)
This image is from a 300-meter typographic pavement built in Morecombe, England. It was created by Why Not Associates, in collaboration with Gordon Young, as part of an arts-based regeneration project for the town. The path features poems, lyrics and traditional sayings set in different typographical styles and built in granite, concrete, steel, brass and glass, which shows that type can be realized in a wide range of materials and settings.

sparow,

nightinga...

swalow,

AND THE COW...

...HORPES LYTE;

VENUS S...

...THAT CLEPETH FORTH THE

MORDRER OF THE FU...

THAT MAKEN H...

WITH HI...

W...

Client: Lancaster City Council
Design: Why Not Associates
and Gordon Young
Typographic summary:
Various styles to present
poems and expressions

turtel,

pecok,

fesaunt,

unkinde;

Typography | Materials

READ THIS BEFORE USING THAT

Client: Topman
Design: The Kitchen
Typographic summary:
Range-left upper case Helvetica Neue and Hoefler Text, concertina insert, lenticular printing

Remember to show your Topman 1hundred Card, accompanied by any form of photo-i-d to a member of Topman staff who will be available to help. For a more pleasurable shopping experience, our team of Trend Advisors can be on hand to assist with anything from locating the right sizes to giving advice on current style trends. If it's a suit you're after, Topman now has Smart Advisors specifically trained to find the right cut and fit for you. There are also VIP changing rooms, complimentary refreshments and even a speed payment service.

To make an appointment with one of our Trend or Smart Advisors, please call 020 7323 0328.

1hundred

Clothing retailer Topman mailed clam boxes containing a motion card and a concertina instruction booklet to 100 key fashion movers and shakers including DJs, models and club owners – the kind of people that the chain wanted to endorse its clothes. The personalized motion card with a lenticular of the recipient's name, ensured that each card was unique, and provided a response to the 'Don't you know who I am?' question that was also printed as a lenticular on the card. A motion card shows depth or motion as the viewing angle changes. The lenticular printing technique alternates strips of several images on to the back of a transparent plastic sheet, which contains a series of curved ridges called lenticules. The strips are aligned so that those forming a specific image are refracted to the same point.

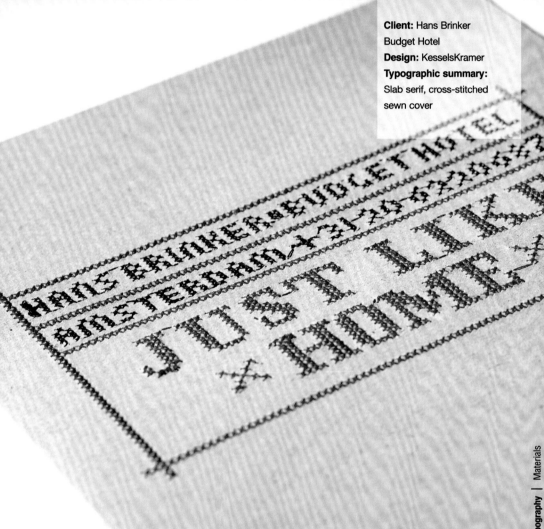

Client: Hans Brinker
Budget Hotel
Design: KesselsKramer
Typographic summary:
Slab serif, cross-stitched
sewn cover

Typography | Materials

Just Like Home

This brochure, by KesselsKramer for Amsterdam's Hans Brinker Budget Hotel, features a cover with typography that has been sewn into the substrate in red and black thread and results in a more tactile and homely piece than the typical printed approach. This stylistic feature is repeated inside the publication as the type is set within cross-stitched borders.

Client: Her House
Design: Studio Myerscough
Typographic summary:
Slab serif type silk-screen
printed on to a wood
substrate

Her House (above)

This invitation created for Her House gallery by Studio Myerscough uses a slab serif typeface that is silk-screened on to a wood substrate. The slab serifs have a punchiness and solidity that distinguishes the characters from the grain of the wood.

Soak (right)

This invitation – to a discussion evening with graphic design company SEA Design – created by Iris Associates does not, at first, appear to have any typography other than the logotype. The characters of this are fashioned from the shapes of liquid droplets in harmony with the process of something becoming soaked.

The logotype also serves as an instruction, by immersing the invitation, the water acts on the dark blue thermographic ink that is screen-printed over the light-blue permanent ink on a rigid white PVC substrate and reveals the details of the event. Rather cleverly 'soak' becomes 'SEA'.

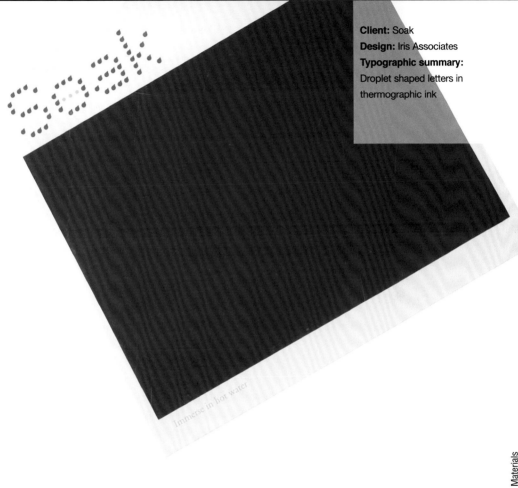

Client: Soak
Design: Iris Associates
Typographic summary:
Droplet shaped letters in
thermographic ink

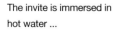

The invite is immersed in
hot water ...

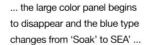

... the large color panel begins
to disappear and the blue type
changes from 'Soak' to SEA' ...

... the central panel fades enough
for the body text of the invitation
to be clearly visible.

Printing techniques

Designers can choose from a range of different printing techniques to put a design on a substrate. Offset lithography is the main printing method used to produce paper-based publications including the majority of designs showcased in this book, and the book itself. However, other techniques such as letterpress, hot metal, silk-screen, block and gravure are available.

Each of these techniques imparts qualities into a design beyond putting the ink on the page, due to the characteristics of the printing technique, such as the pressure used. In this way they can add individuality and uniqueness to a design and/or tactile qualities.

A more recent development is digital printing. This is transforming the design sector by providing the ability to print low volumes economically and single prints, to print in white, print spot varnishes and even print emboss effects where layers are built up. The ability to print low volumes allows designers to return to the craft aspects of the printing tradition and experiment more by creating one-off pieces.

Royal Mail

Pictured is a package designed for Royal Mail by Blast design studio using a letterpress type collage by Alan Kitching. The letterpress characters were pressed into the substrate providing it with tactile qualities and a sense of a past time. The collage reflects the themes for the commemorative stamps issued during the year that the package contains.

Client: Royal Mail
Design: Blast / Alan Kitching
Typographic summary:
Letterpress type collage

Typography | Printing techniques

Letterpress printing

Letterpress is a method of relief printing whereby an inked, raised surface is pressed against the paper. It was the first commercial printing method and is the source of many printing terms. The raised surface that makes the impression is typically made from pieces of type, but photoengraved plates can also be used. A defect of letterpress printing is appealing to modern designers. When improperly inked, patches appear in the letters giving them a uniqueness, where each impression is subtly different.

Client: Ericsson
Design: Imagination
Typographic summary:
Silk-screen printed sans serif
Helvetica, overlayed with a
fine mesh of printed lines

Silk-screen printing
Silk-screen print finishing forces ink through a stencil, pattern or template that has been produced on silk
(or similar cloth), and stretched across a frame. The primary advantage of this printing method is that it can
be used across a wide range of substrates, particularly those that are unsuited to other printing methods.

Making Sense of the New Economy

This invitation, for an event by telecommunications company Ericsson, was designed by Imagination. The theme of the event was the New Economy and the type used on the invitation was in keeping with this.

Helvetica 65, a sans serif typeface with a modern feel, was silk-screen printed on to a transparent acetate substrate. A fine mesh of hairlines was printed on to the front of the invitation and the accompanying material, and the type printed in reverse on the back. The resulting 'layering', conveys a sense of communication and connection with minimum effort. The controlled simplicity of the print material is enhanced by the subtle raised ink offered by the silk-screen process.

Typography | Printing techniques

Print finishing

Print finishing covers a range of techniques that are used to finish a printed piece, often enhancing the typography. Print finishing can enhance the appearance of type through the use of screen printing or colored varnishes for example, or make it more subtle through the use of blind embossing, flocking or spot varnish. The considered use of print finishing can elevate an ordinary piece to something exceptional, as well as enhancing communication.

Architect Mies van der Rohe noted that 'God is in the detail', and this holds true with print finishing as it can communicate, inform and impart information, entertain and excite through the tactile qualities such methods impart into the characters. An embossed book demands not just to be read but also to be felt; the curious shape of a die-cut invitation differentiates it sufficiently for it to be read while other mail remains unopened. Print items can be engineered to elicit a specific response and print-finishing techniques are key to this.

Tine+Chris

Pictured is a wedding invitation created by Triboro for Tine+Chris made from laser cut steel that presents a novel inversion of the typical invitation. Here, the typography is presented without any substrate and is the actual invitation.

Client: Tine+Chris
Design: Triboro
Typographic summary:
Laser cut steel creating
physical letterforms
without backing substrate

Laser cutting

Laser cutting is a print finishing technique that uses a laser to cut voids in a substrate. The high energy of the laser may burn some substrates which can be desirable, or not. Also, when laser cutting typography the bowls of letters such as 'o', 'p' and 'b' fall out.

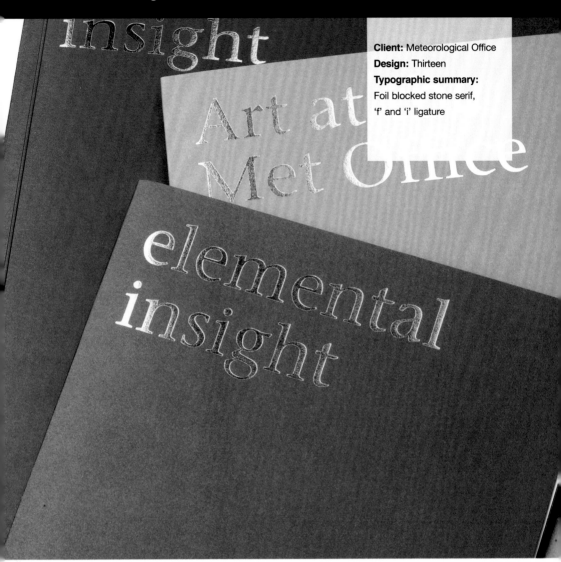

Client: Meteorological Office
Design: Thirteen
Typographic summary:
Foil blocked stone serif,
'f' and 'i' ligature

Art at the Met Office

This catalog was created for the UK's Meteorological Office by Thirteen design studio for a traveling exhibition and features the understated use of a foil blocked stone serif typeface to provide each element with a unified appearance.

Foil blocking

Foil blocking is a finishing technique that applies a colored foil to a substrate via heat transfer. It is typically used to provide gold, copper or silver coloring with a convincing metallic look. Other terms that can be applied to the same process include: foil stamping, heat (or hot) stamping, block stamping or foil embossing.

Client: Royal Mail
Design: Webb & Webb
Typographic summary:
Heavy debossing to
harmonize sculptural theme

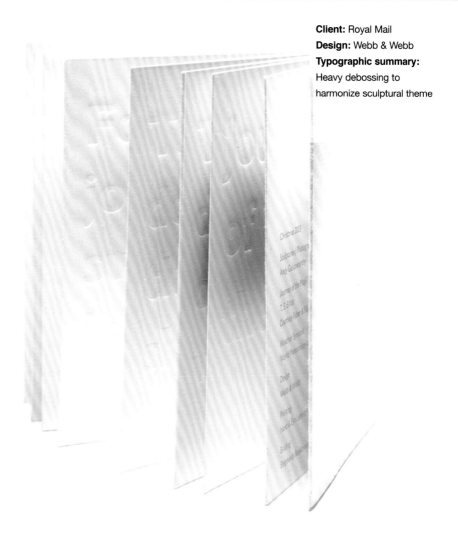

Typography | Print finishing

Royal Mail

This booklet, for Royal Mail by Webb & Webb design studio uses a heavy
substrate that takes a heavy deboss that harmonizes with the sculptural theme
of the series of postage stamps created by sculptor Andy Goldsworthy.

Embossing and debossing

These techniques are used to produce different visual and tactile effects to a design, particularly to the
covers of reports or books, invitations or other identity items. Embossing is a raised effect and debossing
is a recessed effect.

Client: EMI
Design: SEA Design
Typographic summary:
Debossed flock cover

EMI

This cover for an annual report for music company EMI was designed by Sea Design studio. Its solitary feature is the word 'music' debossed into the flock substrate to give a two-tone effect with depth and texture.

Flocking

Flocking is a process that deposits small fibers or flock onto a substrate to provide a tactile, often velvety feel. In design, it can be found on covers and wallpaper.

Client: Esther Franklin
Design: MadeThought
Typographic summary:
UV varnished initials to
create texture

Esther Franklin

This identity for fashion designer Esther Franklin, features her initials (EF) repeated in full-coverage, UV varnish over the design to form a textural pattern on a heavy, matt-black stock.

Typography | Print finishing

Varnishes

Varnish is a liquid shellac, or plastic coating, added to a printed piece after the final ink pass in order to enhance the appearance, texture or durability by sealing the surface. It may add a glossy, satin or dull finish and it can also be tinted to add color. Varnish can be applied either as full coverage or as a spot varnish.

UV varnish is a heavy, high-gloss, matt or satin varnish applied after printing and cured in an ultra-violet dryer.
Spot varnish is applied to highlight specific areas of a printed piece. It brings the colors to life, or it can be used to create subtle textures on the page. It is usually applied as a spot color with an extra printing plate.
Machine varnish is a thin oil-based coat that is applied on a printing press and produces a very light gloss.

Most print finishing processes are performed **offline**, after the job has been printed. All highly visible and textural varnishes need to be applied offline. However, some varnishes may be applied **online** as part of the printing process, normally as an extra color.

Industry view: Graphical House

Type is often a small, but crucial part of a greater whole and it can be the element that coherently draws other design aspects together. This case study features the creation of a three-dimensional item to represent the collection of fashion designer Paul Smith. The subtle type intervention conveys, in few words, both the sense of obliqueness and tailored garments through the creation of a dot typeface that mimics the regularly-spaced holes of a sewing machine.

What are the principal challenges of creating and producing type on objects such as the Paul Smith Oblique dominoes?

The challenges depend very much on the specific nature of the object. In this case we were only rendering the type on the packaging for the dominoes rather than the pieces themselves, so in that respect it was relatively straightforward and like any other print production job. Having said that it was very important that there was a direct connection between the object and the logotype. This is reflected not only within the typeface design but also in the production. The type is foil-blocked, the indentation created by the block provides a tactile reference to the drilled dots of the dominoes themselves. The challenge of the dominoes was far greater as each dot was drilled and finished by hand.

What is it about typography that lends itself to becoming such a focal point of a brand image that other design elements, like images often do not have?

At its core typography is simple and flexible but it communicates directly. It is possible to imbue ideas within a logotype and therefore within the brand name itself. Type is easy to reproduce on any kind of surface, in any media. It works in one color, it can be printed, carved or drawn with a biro on your school bag. It is simple to take ownership of, both as a brand but also as a consumer. Type sits at the heart of most brands as the most fundamental expression.

The dominoes with hand-drilled holes.

Industry view | Graphical House

Where do you find inspiration to create innovative type interventions in a design?

Inspiration comes from all kinds of places, just the same with type as with anything else. Naturally primary inspiration comes from within the project itself. In finding ways to express some of the ideas and values within the typography itself. Sometimes the difficulty is keeping hold of the reins and making sure things don't go too far, that the simplicity and clarity is retained.

The Oblique production was more complex than a typical print job and getting it wrong could be very expensive to rectify. What advice would you give a young designer to ensure that they do not make expensive mistakes when producing a physical type realization? What are the key things to get right?

Expensive mistakes will be made. Take risks but minimize them as far as possible. Prototyping is essential, even if it's a scruffy paper and sticky tape sample. Make it physical to see if it works. It's amazing how much something changes in the transition from screen to a physical object. If you are considering unusual production techniques, things that maybe haven't been done before, then suppliers are often happy to advise or even try things out if they aren't sure what will work either. If you take risks, sometimes they don't pay off; it's all about using your knowledge and experience to understand what can be done, not simply because it has been done, but because you know how the medium works.

Graphical House is a design consultancy based in Glasgow, Scotland that produces beautifully crafted work across all applications from digital and analog to environmental.

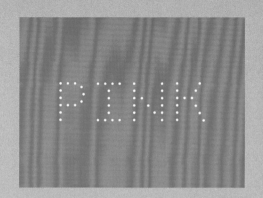

The box of dominoes packaging with type that mimics clothing stitching and the holes on the dominoes.

Industry view | Graphical House

Exercises

The exercises that follow are derived from ISTD (International Society of Typographic Designers) student assessment briefs in recent years. As with all ISTD student briefs there is a strong focus on content and research, and how this can be translated into typographic solutions. The briefs and their solutions presented here are intended to give an individual the parameters to work within, while often (but not always) passing authorship over to the student.

Typography is a vehicle for language so the content that you choose is as important as how you choose to interpret it. Here you can see how various students responded to these briefs.

Exercise 1 A Life's Work
Author John Paul Dowling for Linotype

A Life's Work

The day Ottmar Mergenthaler demonstrated the first linecasting machine to the *New York Tribune* in 1886, Whitelaw Reid, the editor, was delighted: 'Ottmar,' he said, 'you've cast a line of type!' The editor's words formed the basis for the company label and marked the beginning of Linotype's success story. Four years later, the ingenious inventor founded the Mergenthaler Linotype Company. For more than 100 years, the Linotype name was synonymous with high quality typefaces. In 2006, Linotype GmbH was acquired by Monotype Imaging Holdings Inc, and in 2013 was renamed Monotype GmbH. The Linotype library remains part of the Monotype libraries and continues as an active type label. Linotype.com also remains a thriving e-commerce portal through which you can obtain the latest Linotype typefaces as well as the font products of other libraries and font foundries.

Adrian Frutiger, who passed away in September 2015, was a Swiss typeface designer who influenced the direction of digital typography in the second half of the 20th century and into the 21st. His career spanned the hot metal, phototypesetting and digital typesetting eras.

Frutiger's most famous designs – Univers, Frutiger and Avenir – are landmark sans serif families spanning the three main genres of sans-serif typefaces: neo-grotesque, humanist and geometric. Univers was notable for being one of the first sans serif faces to form a consistent but wide-ranging family across a range of widths and weights. Frutiger described creating sans serif types as his 'main life's work'.

Brief

Celebrate the life's work of Adrian Frutiger. Create a prestigious 'publication' (digital/physical or both) that celebrates the life and work of Adrian Frutiger. You may wish to compare/contrast his type designs or look to explore current events of the time in society, culture and politics for example. Explore opportunities to contextualize your subject and his work. For example, consider biographical, literary, cultural and historical reference points to inform visual content and typographic interpretation.

This publication should be special as it will pay homage to one of the world's great type designers and so it should be designed, produced and presented accordingly.

Typography | Exercises

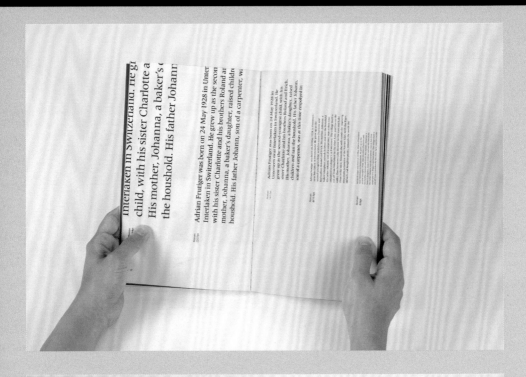

Shown is work by Chia-Lin Lin, London College of Communication, celebrating and paying homage to the achievements and typeface designs of Adrian Frutiger.

Exercise 2 Milestones
Author John Paul Dowling, National College of Art & Design, Dublin

Milestones

Since Roman times a milestone has been one of a series of numbered markers placed along a road or boundary at intervals of one mile or occasionally, parts of a mile. Milestones are constructed to provide reference points along a route and reassure travelers that the proper path is being followed, and to indicate the distance traveled from or remaining to a destination.

The term is also used to describe key moments in our lives, the history of our planet, historical events that have unfolded over time, or steps towards a goal. The term can also be used in reference to emotional growth, stages of learning or any such topic to show the element of progression.

Brief

Choose a person or subject that has existed for a significant number of years and produce a body of work that gives a reader greater insight into your area of research and how milestones have played a role in the existence of the subject matter, whether good or bad. You may choose to focus on one particular milestone, or a series of milestones that are connected in some way.

A milestone, like a rite of passage, can be used to explore and describe various points in an individual's life such as for any marked transitional stage when one's social status is altered. Rites of passage show anthropologists what social hierarchies, values and beliefs are important in specific cultures. Be inventive with your subject matter, avoid the obvious, explore the obscure, and highlight the unseen. You must consider what is important to your intended audience and deliver the content in the most appropriate format(s).

This.

angered.

Jeffrey.

Once again, he was left feeling alone, unwanted and lost.

Jeffrey saw this as abandonm

...her ended up getting custody of David, a ...members in Chippewa Falls, Wisco

...his father was no

Shown is work by Muhammad Gangat, University of Johannesburg, exploring through typography the life and death of Jeffrey Dahmer.

Exercise 3 Visualizing Music
Author Barrie Tullett, University
of Lincoln

Experimental music scores have long attempted to offer an alternative to more formal 'staff' notation. John Cage, Steve Reich, Brian Eno, Cornelius Cardew, Hans-Christoph Steiner, Gyorgy Ligeti, Tom Phillips... the list of artists and musicians trying to find a different way of expressing music is considerable.

Brief
Using Philip Glass' opera *Einstein on the Beach* as your source material, investigate different ways of making visual typographic notations in order to create a music score for this work that can be performed without reference to traditional staff notation of five horizontal lines and four spaces.

Consider a more avant-garde approach, one that is often found in graphic scores, oramics or eye music that represent music through the use of visual symbols outside the realm of traditional music notation.

Remember that your typographic response will be a score for a performance. It is not free form jazz. While there can be some aspect of interpretation, the final piece must adhere to a rigorous internal logic.

Whether the piece is to be performed by professionals or amateurs is up to you. Whether it is to be performed by people who have heard the opera or not is up to you. Whether it is to be performed by people who can read music or not is up to you. Whether these things matter or not is up to you.

Typography | Exercises

This is about Music and Numbers

Shown is work by Jennifer O'Brien, National College of Art & Design, Dublin. Using the music from Philip Glass' opera *Einstein on the Beach*, this book visually investigates the layers of melody, rhythm, numerics and text and highlights the harmony within the music to give the reader a better understanding of the opera itself.

Exercise 4 It Happened On This Day Author Barrie Tullett, University of Lincoln

I recently discovered that I share a birthdate with the BBC broadcasting its first televised news bulletin; the Salvation Army being founded in London's East End; Spam being introduced and, not least, the birth of 'Dolly the Sheep'. Subsequently, to find that I share a birthday with PT Barnum, Robbie Robertson, Paul Smith, Huey Lewis and Royce da 5'9" inspired the widest range of emotions and aspiration.

Access to data is so effective that we are now better equipped than ever to create information that expresses histories in the personal as well as international forum.

The Brief
Consider how best to interpret the project theme. Is it what happened through the centuries on a specific day in a month/year or could it be the story of one particular day in time? The 'Big Bang'; Battle of Hastings; the first pulls of Gutenberg's 42-line Bible'; Elvis Presley on the Ed Sullivan Show; the assassination of JFK; Liverpool's European Cup win in 2005 or the atrocity of 9/11 – you are spoilt for choice.

However fascinating the topic and the information that you select is, your challenge is to create a delivery platform that demands the reader's attention. It needs to address the norms of information architecture while actively working to evoke an emotional response from the reader or viewer. Use print, screen, combined media – the choice is yours – as long as it expresses a solid idea, informs us and shows your typographic skills. Remember that words and language are our collateral and that your submission should be essentially typographic.

Typography | Exercises

Shown is *OMG in the OED* by Magnus Hearn, University of the West of England. A compilation of some of the words that were added to the Oxford English Dictionary on March 24th 2011. March's update was 2011's first quarterly update and contains some of the most interesting, outrageous and controversial entries in recent years.

Apex

The point formed at the top of a character such as 'A' where the left and right strokes meet.

Arm

See Bar.

Ascender

The part of a letter that extends above the x-height.

Bar

The horizontal stroke on characters 'A', 'H', 'T', 'e', 'f', 't'. Sometimes called a crossbar on 'A' and 'H' or an arm on 'F', 'T', 'E' and 'K' upstroke.

Baseline

The baseline is an imaginary line upon which a line of text sits and is the point from which other elements of type are measured including x-height and leading.

Bezier curve

A curve created by two terminal points and two or more control points for a letter shape.

Bicapitalization

Non-standard capitalization where compound words or phrases that are joined without spacing are capitalized.

Bitmap

An image that is composed of dots.

Blackletter

A typeface based on the ornate writing prevalent during the Middle Ages. Also called Block,

Gothic, Old English, Black or Broken.

Body text

Body text or copy is the text that forms the main part of a work. It is usually between 8 and 14 points in size.

Bold

A version of the Roman with a wider stroke. Also called medium, semi-bold, black, super or poster.

Boldface type

A thick, heavy variety of type used to give emphasis.

Bowl

The stroke that surrounds and contains the counter.

Bracket

The curved portion of a serif that connects it to the stroke.

Camel case

See bicapitalization.

Character

An individual element of type such as a letter or punctuation mark.

Chin

The terminal angled part of the 'G'.

Condensed

A narrower version of the roman cut.

Counter

The empty space inside the body stroke surrounded by the bowl.

Cross stroke

Horizontal stroke that crosses over the stem.

Crossbar

See Bar.

Crotch

Where the leg and arm of the 'K' and 'k' meet.

Deboss

A design stamped without ink or foil recessed into the substrate.

Descender

The part of a letter that extends below the baseline.

Die cut

Special shapes cut into a substrate by a steel rule.

Display type

Large and/or distinctive type intended to attract the eye. Specifically cut to be viewed from a distance.

Down stroke

The heavy stroke in a type character.

Drop capital

A capital letter set in a larger point size and aligned with the top of the first line.

Ear

Decorative flourish on the upper right side of the 'g' bowl.

Em

Unit of measurement derived from the width of the square body of the cast upper case 'M'. An em equals the size of a given type ie the em of 10 point type is 10 points.

Emboss
A design stamped without ink or foil giving a raised surface.

En
Unit of measurement equal to half of one em.

Extended
A wider version of the Roman cut.

Extender
The part of a letter that extends above the x-height (ascender) or that falls below the base line (descender).

Eye
A name specifically given to the counter of an 'e'.

Font
The physical attributes needed to make a typeface be it film, metal, wood or PostScript information.

Foot
Serif at the bottom of the stem that sits on the baseline.

Flock
A speciality cover paper produced by coating the sheet with a dyed flock powder (very fine woollen refuse or vegetable fibre dust). Originally intended to simulate tapestry and Italian velvet brocade.

Geometric
Sans serif typefaces that are based on geometric shapes identifiable by round 'O' and 'Q' letters.

Golden section
A division in the ratio 8:13 that produces harmonious proportions.

Gothic
A typeface without serifs. Also called sans serif or lineale.

Gravure
A high volume intaglio printing process in which the printing area is etched into the printing plate.

Hairline
The thinnest stroke in a typeface that has varying widths. Also refers to a 0.25pt line, the thinnest line that can be confidently produced by printing processes.

Hand drawn
Typography that is hand made.

Hierarchy
A logical, organized and visual guide for text headings that indicate different levels of importance.

Hook
Serif at the top of a stem.

Ink trapping
The adjustment of areas of color, text or shapes to account for mis-registration on the printing press by overlapping them.

Intercaps
See bicapitalization.

Italic
A version of the roman cut that angles to the right at 7-20 degrees.

Kerning
The removal of unwanted space between letters.

Kerning pairs
Letter combinations that frequently need to be kerned.

Knockout
Where an underlying color has a gap inserted where another color would overprint it. The bottom color is knocked out to prevent color mixing.

Leading
The space between lines of type measured from baseline to baseline. It is expressed in points and is a term derived from hot-metal printing when strips of lead were placed between lines of type to provide line spacing.

Leg
The lower, down-sloping stroke of the 'K', 'k' and 'R'. Sometimes used for the tail of a 'Q'.

Legibility
The ability to distinguish one letter from another due to characteristics inherent in the typeface design.

Lenticular
A printed image that shows depth or motion as the viewing angle changes. Also called motion card.

Ligatures
The joining of two or three separate characters to form a single unit to avoid interference between certain letter combinations.

Light / thin
A version of the roman cut with a lighter stroke.

Lining figures
Lining figures are numerals that share the same height and rest on the baseline.

Link
The part that joins the two counters of the double-storey 'g'.

Loop
The enclosed or partially enclosed lower counter in a Roman, i.e. double-storey 'g'. Sometimes used to describe the cursive 'p' and 'b'.

Lowercase
See Minuscules.

Majuscules
Capital letters. Also called uppercase.

Meanline
Imaginary line that runs across the tops of non-ascending characters

Measure
The length of a line of text expressed in picas.

Minuscule
Characters originated from the Carolingian letters. Also called lowercase.

Monospaced
Where each character occupies a space with the same width.

Oblique
A slanted version of roman whose letterforms are essentially those of the Roman form. Mistakenly called 'italics'.

Old style
Old style, Antiqua, Ancient, Renaissance, Baroque, Venetian or Garalde is a typeface style developed by Renaissance typographers that was based on Roman inscriptions. It was created to replace the blackletter type and is characterized by low stroke contrast, bracketed serifs, and a left-inclining stress.

Old style figures
Numerals that vary in height and do not sit on the same baseline.

Overprint
Where one printing ink is printed over another printing ink.

Paths
A mathematical statement that defines a vector graphic object.

Pica
A measurement for specifying line lengths. One pica is 12 points (UK/US) or 4.22mm. There are six picas to an inch.

Point system
The measurement for specifying typographical dimensions. The British and American point is 1/72 of an inch. The European Didot system provides similar size values.

PostScript
A page description language used by laser printers and on-screen graphics systems.

Readability
The overall visual representation of the text narrative.

Roman
The basic letterform.

Rotogravure
See Gravure.

Sans serif
A typeface without decorative serifs. Typically with little stroke thickness variation, a larger x-height and no stress in rounded strokes.

Script
A typeface designed to imitate handwriting.

Serif
A small stroke at the end of a main vertical or horizontal stroke. Also used as a classification for

fonts that contain such decorative rounded, pointed, square, or slab serif finishing strokes.

Shoulder or body
The arch formed on the 'h'.

Slab serif
A fonts with heavy, squared off finishing strokes, low contrast and few curves.

Small caps
Small caps are majuscules that are close in size to the minuscules of a given typeface. They are less domineering than regular size capitals and are used setting acronyms and common abbreviations.

Spine
The left to right curving stroke in 'S' and 's'.

Spur or cat's ear
The end of the curved part of 'C' or 'S'.

Stem
The main vertical or diagonal stroke of a letter.

Stock
The paper or other substrate to be printed upon.

Stress
The direction in which a curved stroke changes weight.

Stroke
The diagonal portion of letterforms such as 'N', 'M', or 'Y'. Stems, bars, arms, bowls etc. are collectively referred to as strokes.

Substrate
Any surface or material that is to be printed upon.

Surprint
See Overprint.

Tail
Descending stroke on 'Q', 'K' or 'R'. Descenders on 'g', 'j', 'p', 'q', and 'y' may also be called tails.

Terminal
A curve such as a tail, link, ear or loop, also called a finial. A ball terminal combines a tail dot or circular stroke with a hook at the end of a tail or arm. A beak terminal is a sharp spur at the end of an arm.

Text
Written or printed matter that forms the body of a publication.

Tracking
The adjustable amount of space between letters.

TrueType
Fonts specified with bezier curves outlines.

Typeface
The letters, numbers and punctuation marks of a type design.

Typeface family
A series of typefaces sharing common characteristics but with different sizes and weights.

Type styles
The different visual appearances of typefaces.

Uppercase
See Majuscules.

Upstroke
The finer stroke of a type character.

Varnish
Coating applied to a printed sheet for protection or appearance.

Vector graphic
A scalable object created by paths.

Vertex
The angle formed at the bottom where the left and right strokes meet such as with the 'V'.

X-height
The height of the lowercase 'x' of a given typeface.

Typography | Glossary

Acknowledgments and Picture Credits

While a lot seems to have changed or advanced in the ten years since we produced the first edition of this book, it is important to question whether things have changed as much as we think they have. The basic principles of good design remain as the foundation upon which to build creatively and much of the work featured in the first edition has stood the test of time and remains as relevant today as it was ten years ago. The digital space has advanced exponentially placing new demands on designers for solutions that can harness such progress. The techniques may have changed but the principles remain.

We would like to thank everyone who supported us during the creation of this second edition including the many art directors, designers and creative who showed great generosity in allowing us to reproduce their work. Special thanks to everyone who hunted for, collated, compiled and rediscovered some of the fascinating work contained in this book.

Thanks to Xavier Young for his patience, determination and skill in photographing the work showcased in this book and to Heather Marshall for modelling. And a final big thanks to Lesley Ripley, Georgia Kennedy and the team at Bloomsbury Visual Arts.

Photography by Xavier Young pp 25, 27, 35, 55, 57, 59, 61, 85, 89, 113, 117, 120, 129, 137, 160, 164, 165, 166, 167, 170, 171, 174, 175, 176, 177

Typography | Acknowledgments and Picture Credits

Page numbers in *italics* refer to captions.

Typography | Index